Praise for
The Secret Lives of Toddlers

"A must read for all parents of young children and everyone who loves 'small' people. This is a delightful and valuable book. Highly recommended."
—Richard Carlson,
author of *Don't Sweat the Small Stuff . . . and It's All Small Stuff*

"Delightfully written, *The Secret Lives of Toddlers* shows us the everyday magic in our children's lives, highlighting their imagination and sense of discovery. With expert testimonials and parental advice learned on-the-job, these bite-sized chapters help us smile more and appreciate why PLAY=LEARNING." —Kathy Hirsh-Pasek, Ph.D. Temple University, author of *Einstein Never Used Flashcards* and *How Babies Talk*

"This is a breakthrough parenting book! Ms. Murphy provides valuable information that satisfies our need to understand our childrens' behavior, and in addition she gives fabulous practical approaches for dealing with toddlers—all in everyday language and a concise parent-friendly format. A must read (and great gift) for all parents of toddlers." —Carol Kline, coauthor, *Chicken Soup for the Mother's Soul 2*

"As a pediatrician, I am often asked by parents why their children act the way they do. I used to explain puzzling behaviors and then comment, 'It's a shame children aren't delivered with instruction manuals in their little hands!' Jana Murphy has written a user-friendly guide for parents of children ages 1 to 3 that treats both toddlers and their parents with respect and understanding. It's very close to my ideal instruction guide for this age group. Any parent of a toddler or preschooler would find daily life easier by consulting this book." —Lynn Mowbray Wegner, M.D., F.A.A.P.
Developmental/Behavioral Pediatrician
chairperson, the American Academy of Pediatrics Section
on Developmental and Behavioral Pediatrics
Learning and Development Associates, Morrisville, NC

THE SECRET LIVES OF
Toddlers

*A Parent's Guide
to the Wonderful,
Terrible, Fascinating
Behavior of Children
Ages 1 to 3*

Jana Murphy

A PERIGEE BOOK

Author's Note

Out of respect for all the parents of toddlers who may not have time to read a book from start to finish for years to come, each chapter in *The Secret Lives of Toddlers* is designed to work with or without the rest of the text. For this reason, experts who provided information are introduced by their full names and with their credentials in each chapter in which they are quoted.

A Perigee Book
Published by The Berkley Publishing Group
A division of Penguin Group (USA) Inc.
375 Hudson Street
New York, New York 10014

First Perigee paperback edition: October 2004

ISBN: 0-399-53023-1

Visit our website at
www.penguin.com

Library of Congress Cataloging-in-Publication Data

Murphy, Jana.
    The secret lives of toddlers / Jana Murphy.—1st Perigee pbk. ed.
      p. cm.
    "A Perigee book."
    ISBN 0-399-53023-1 (pbk.)
    1. Toddlers.   I. Title.
HQ774.5.M86 2004
305.232—dc22   2004044571

Printed in the United States of America
10 9 8 7 6 5 4 3 2 1

For Brendan, Matilda, and Connor,
quite possibly the three most adorable toddlers ever.

Acknowledgments

The Secret Lives of Toddlers is only possible because the experts in each of the fields explored were willing to share their expertise. My sincerest gratitude goes to the following people for taking time out of their busy schedules to answer my questions and share their knowledge.

Diane Beals, Ed.D., University of Tulsa
Michael Bye, M.D., Columbia University College of Medicine and Surgery
Angela Camasto, M.D., Kids First Pediatrics in Easton, Pennsylvania
Gregory Dean, M.D., Temple University School of Medicine
Marian Diamond, Ph.D., University of California at Berkeley
Lisabeth DiLalla, Ph.D., Southern Illinois University School of Medicine
Martha Farrell Erickson, Ph.D., University of Minnesota
Jennifer Fisher, Ph.D., Baylor College of Medicine
Stephanie Gottwald, MA, Tufts University
Paul Harris, Ph.D., Harvard University
Ellen Hock, Ph.D., Ohio State University at Columbus
Alice Sterling Honig, Ph.D., Syracuse University
Mary Hynes-Berry, Ph.D., Erikson Institute for Early Childhood

Tovah Klein, Ph.D., Barnard College

Laurie Kramer, Ph.D., University of Illinois at Urbana

Kang Lee, Ph.D., University of California at San Diego

Megan McClelland, Ph.D., Oregon State University

Joan Brooks McLane, Ph.D., Erikson Institute for Early Childhood

Jodi Mindell, Ph.D., St. Joseph's University, Philadelphia

Susan Nelson, M.D., University of Memphis Medical School

Jane Perry, Ph.D., University of California at Berkeley

Michael Potegal, Ph.D., University of Minnesota

Dorothy Richmond, M.D., Georgetown University

Mark Strauss, Ph.D., University of Pittsburgh

Marjorie Taylor, Ph.D., University of Oregon

Teri Turner, M.D., Baylor College of Medicine

Jo Ellen Vespo, Ph.D., Utica College

DeDe Wohlfarth, Psy.D., Spalding University

Harriet Worobey, Rutgers University

This book would never have been possible without the encouragement and guidance of agent Jeff Kleinman at the Graybill & English Literary Agency. Thank you for your patience, support, and professionalism. Thank you to Sheila Curry Oakes at Perigee for seeing the potential in a book like this, and for wanting me to hurry up and write it so she could better understand her own toddler. Thanks also to John Duff, publisher of Perigee, Sally Franklin for her careful copyediting, and to the members of the publicity department for putting their enthusiasm into helping this book find its audience.

My sincere gratitude goes to Dr. Edward Christophersen, who shares my deep admiration for the unique joys of life with toddlers, and who provided priceless insight and encouragement.

The idea for *The Secret Lives of Toddlers* came from the toddlers who have graced my own life. I can't thank my nieces, my nephews, and my own children enough for being so loving, puzzling, wonderful, terrible, and inspiring. It is one of the great privileges of my life to be surrounded by such a remarkable group of kids. I thank my parents and grandparents, too, for raising me in an environment where children were always treasured.

Thanks most of all to John, who said we could live on macaroni and cheese if I couldn't make a living as a writer, and who pushed me to write about the things that matter to me. Your love makes me feel like I can do anything.

Contents

PART IV: THIS LITTLE BODY OF MINE

Foreword

When I first spoke with Jana Murphy about *The Secret Lives of Toddlers*, I told her there's more educational value to be had in spending an afternoon watching a good mother with her children than in anything I could say in an interview. When the manuscript for this book landed on my desk, I realized that Jana is just the kind of mom I was talking about. Every page of her book bears the stamp of a parent who has been there. Even more compelling than the perspective of a parent who has shared your experience, though, is getting a rare glimpse at the world through the eyes of the toddlers themselves. Through a close review of the relevant research and extensive interviews with experts in toddler behavior, psychology, and pediatrics, *The Secret Lives of Toddlers* helps parents understand why toddlers do the things they do, and how we can deter negative behaviors, encourage positive ones, and accept the things that are simply rights of passage for early childhood.

As parents, we usually read books about children to confirm that we're on the right track, and to get another person's take on how to approach interesting, difficult or frustrating behaviors from our children. *The Secret Lives of Toddlers* is excellent in both respects. Jana Murphy looks at the issues we face everyday as parents and peels away the layers of confusion and mystery, explaining why toddlers do things like play with the box and not the gift, or insist on eating only macaroni for days. She provides practical suggestions for the issues we perceive to be difficult, and she adds some much needed humor and perspective to her discussion of issues that many parents of toddlers find frustrating.

This isn't a textbook that has to be read from cover to cover while taking notes. Rather, it's a rich compendium of information about all things toddler. There's an informative, readable mix of descriptions of behaviors and research on them that never sounds overly academic or dramatic. There's also a consistent and familiar format throughout the book that makes it easy to read and easy to find what you're looking for. Many parents of toddlers just don't have the luxury of sitting down to read their parenting books from front to back. *The Secret Lives of Toddlers* is equally informative and enjoyable when you're reading from start to finish or just looking for a quick pep talk and suggestions on a single topic.

Reading *The Secret Lives of Toddlers* will make most parents feel good about themselves and their ability to live through, accept, change, enjoy, and redirect their toddlers' behavior. In many ways, this book is like a smart, experienced mom who lives next door. Easy to read, factual, research based, encouraging, and packed with hundreds of suggestions for everything from circumventing a toddler's temper tantrum to getting through the trials of playdates, sleepless nights, and toilet training, *The Secret Lives of Toddler*s is going to be a staple on the bookshelves of parents of toddlers for a very long time to come.

Edward R. Christophersen, Ph.D.
Children's Mercy Hospital, Kansas City, Missouri,
Author of *Parenting That Works*

Introduction

There are times when just knowing why is enough. If you know the driver racing past you is speeding to the hospital with a sick passenger, you don't curse him for being reckless. If you know your grandma wrapped up the scarf you sent her last year and gave it back for your birthday because her memory is failing, it doesn't hurt your feelings. If you know your husband hid the credit card bill not because he's hiding his latest hi-tech purchase, but because he doesn't want you to know what he's giving you for Christmas—well, who could be mad at that?

Life with toddlers is full of why's—the ones they ask, and the ones they make you ask yourself. "Why would he do that?" is as much a staple of conversation between parents of toddlers as "Boy, I bet you're tired today," and "I think it's your turn."

Researching this book confirmed what I suspected: most of the seemingly inexplicable, mysterious, confusing, frustrating, and adorable things toddlers do come from sensible, rational motivations. Sometimes your toddler can tell you why. More often, they don't understand it themselves, because the logic is physical, or because it comes from a mental or psychological place a toddler couldn't begin to grasp well enough to explain. In many cases, your toddler's behavior is what it is because his cognitive abilities are still growing—he's between a baby and a big kid, and he has far to go in reaching his potential in everything from his social skills and physical prowess to his use of the five senses.

Raising a toddler requires walking a fine line between being lenient and punitive, overindulgent and stifling, cautious and overbearing. No matter how you manage to straddle that line, though, the key to pulling it all together—and having and holding both your toddler's respect and her love—is to begin with a foundation of understanding and affection. I hope this book brings you a little of each. Before you know it, your little enigma is going to speak well, eat without making a mess, face new challenges without hiding behind your legs, and get that unpredictable, roller-coaster ride of a body under control.

When that happens, you may be surprised to discover how much there is to miss in all the interpreting, cajoling, consoling, and even cleaning up that come with having a toddler in your life. There's just something wonderful about having someone who needs you so much— I'm still not sure I understand why.

THE SECRET LIVES OF TODDLERS

*A Parent's Guide to the Wonderful, Terrible,
Fascinating Behavior of Children Ages 1 to 3*

part one

The Way We Play

Chapter 1

WHY DO TODDLERS INSIST ON WEARING THE SAME CLOTHES EVERY DAY?

On Monday, two-year-old Matilda wears her pink sundress, yellow kneesocks (pulled up to her knees, of course), and red sandals. On Tuesday, she chooses the same eye-catching ensemble. On Wednesday, though her mom insists the dress is permanently stained with chocolate syrup, Matilda wins and wears the whole outfit again.

Although Mom is sick of seeing the raggedy dress, she washes it faithfully every night, and she stealthily buys another pair of yellow kneesocks when one of the originals disappears. She's already seen the terror her toddler can be when that favorite outfit is lost in the wash—and she doesn't want to see it again.

Some toddlers get wrestled into their clothes while taking care of important business in the toy box or watching their favorite TV show. They couldn't care less what you dress them in—or if you dress them at all.

Then there are those for whom clothes matter very much. Usually toddlers who want to wear the same clothes day after day aren't doing it to make a fashion statement, explains DeDe Wohlfarth, Psy.D., a clinical psychologist and assistant professor of psychology at Spalding University. They're treating themselves to the fashion equivalent of comfort food.

"The world can feel overwhelming to toddlers because so much is new and unfamiliar. Most of us feel that way, really, but by the time we reach adulthood we learn to adjust to change and accept it," explains Dr. Wohlfarth. "Some toddlers help themselves cope with all the things they *can't* control by placing a great deal of importance on the few things they do have some say in."

Unfortunately, when you're one, or two, or three, there aren't a lot of issues you can control—many toddlers' sphere of influence boils down to the most intimate issues of their own bodies: what they will and will not eat, when they will or will not use the potty, and what they're willing to wear. No wonder that they decide to take those areas of control very seriously.

Any child can decide to latch on to an item of clothing like it's their salvation, but children with parents who agonize over their own wardrobes are particularly prone to it, points out Jo Ellen Vespo, Ph.D., professor of psychology and child life at Utica College. "Toddlers are very astute observers, and identify strongly with their parents—especially the same-sex parent. If Mom makes a big production about choosing her clothes, her daughter may do so as well." And if Dad is the fashion plate in the family, his attentive son may take his wardrobe equally seriously.

No matter where your toddler comes by her strong feelings about what she wants to wear, try not to let it become a big issue between you. At this age, it's a healthy sign that your toddler is making progress toward independence. Save your battles on the clothing front for the years when her friends are sporting micro-minis and green hair.

NOW THAT YOU KNOW

Can you ride it out? So you hate the pink dress. Are you really too embarrassed by it to be seen with your toddler? "The clothing battle is one that many parents are willing to lose," explains Dr. Wohlfarth. "If my toddler has to wear the Thomas the Train t-shirt every day to feel a little better about the world, I don't see why I shouldn't let him." Either the shirt will fall apart or the toddler will outgrow it, but either way this is a problem that will eventually resolve itself.

The toddler uniform. If you can't stand the idea of your toddler in the same shirt every day, and she can't stand the thought of wearing anything else, consider picking up a duplicate outfit. At least you'll have an easier time keeping it clean if you have two.

How does it feel? Before you judge your toddler for her persnickety taste in clothes, take a hard look at what you are asking her to wear when *you* choose. If your selections feature snaps, buttons, or zippers, or if the fabric or cut of the clothes is uncomfortable, you may find that the heart of this matter for your toddler is even more basic than control. More often than not, a toddler's favorite, can't-live-without-it outfit is something that feels nice—a velvet dress, a light cotton t-shirt, or a big, soft pair of sweats, for example. If your toddler's favorite clothes are the most comfortable ones, try to keep that in mind as you choose additions to her wardrobe.

Timing is everything. Any toddler who insists on wearing a single item of clothing because it makes her feel more in control is going to have times when this matters more than others. If your toddler is a grump about changing clothes first thing in the morning, for example, try putting on a clean t-shirt for the next day after a nighttime bath instead. Eliminating that battle at the time when it's the worst can help make matters of wardrobe selection less stressful for both of you.

Let's make a deal. Sometimes letting your toddler have a say in choosing a replacement item or two can make a big difference in how accepting she is of a new outfit. Whether you take your child to her own closet to give her fashion options or take her shopping to pick out something new, be sure she feels like she has some control over what she'll be wearing in the end. Don't try to introduce a whole new wardrobe to a toddler at once—just one or two new items in the rotation will be enough of an adjustment.

Beware the disappearing act. If you're thinking of throwing away the offending clothing item while your toddler is sleeping, give it careful consideration. "Toddlers are really just learning how to define themselves as separate people from their parents," explains Dr. Vespo, "and one of the ways they do that is through their possessions." If you're going to try to eliminate a favorite clothing item, first try slowly working it out of the daily dressing options. For instance, take advantage of a change in the weather to put away an item that might not be warm or cool enough for a couple days, and see how the short period of time goes.

Change of form or function. Sometimes offering an alternative usage for an article of clothing that has become too worn or small for your toddler can make the transition easier. Offer to help your child make a doll dress or a pillow from the favorite clothing item. That way, your toddler will feel as if she has a say in the fate of the item, and she'll have it to hold even after it has become impossible to wear.

Mother/daughter, father/son. If you think your child's attachment to a certain shirt or dress stems from an interest in clothes she's picked up from you, try offering a matching outfit as a substitute. You can buy matching mother/daughter and father/son outfits, but it's easier and less expensive to try matches like blue overalls and red t-shirts from each of your closets instead. Sometimes the novelty of dressing like Mom, Dad, a sibling, or a friend piques a toddler's interest enough to ease her out of her favorite clothing item—at least long enough for you to wash it.

Chapter 2

WHY DO TODDLERS LOVE TO DRESS UP?

Sometimes a hat is all it takes to make a cowboy, firefighter, fairy princess, or pumpkin out of the average toddler. Playing dress-up is one of the oldest rights of passage for young children. It starts as early as before age two, and it lasts for years thereafter. In fact, some of us continue to play as adults—taking pleasure dressing up in our roles as mom or dad, professionals in the business world, and once in a while, if we're lucky, pretty lady and handsome fellow who go out for a fancy dinner.

"I think human beings readily imagine what it would be like to be someone else," explains Paul Harris, Ph.D., professor of education at Harvard Graduate School of Education and author of *The Work of the Imagination*. "As adults, we do this when we read a novel or watch a film. Children—and some adults—do it more actively via role-playing."

There are few methods of imitation more overt than putting on a costume, mimicking a voice, and trying to assume the physical attributes and personality of someone else. In its simplest form, dressing up includes toddlers putting on their parents' clothes or accessories and trying to do some of the things they see us do (one of my nephews, at twenty-two months, put on Mommy's apron, grabbed a broom, dipped it in the dog's water, and proceeded to "clean" the windows). Of course, dress-up can be much more elaborate, with kids pretending to be characters they've seen on television or in the movies, or animals, aliens, or creatures they dream up themselves.

"Toddlers learn by watching and imitating," says Martha Farrell Erickson, Ph.D., Senior Fellow of the Children, Youth and Family Consortium at the University of Minnesota. "They mimic both real people and fantasy characters, but because they are so very physical, dressing up is an appealing way for them to think about what it would be like to be someone else."

While your toddler is imitating you or someone else, you often have a rare opportunity to see what's going on in their impressionable minds. Watch what your toddler does when he's wearing something of yours, pretending to be you, and see which of the things you say is making a lasting impression. Parents are sometimes shocked to hear their own words coming out of their toddlers' mouths. For example, a statement like, "I told you to eat your peas," doesn't sound so bad when you deliver it, but when your toddler repeats it to her dolly, complete with a threatening shove and an evil sneer, you may realize that you're making more of an impact than intended when you ask her to clean her plate.

Even when your toddler takes on an unpleasant character in dress-up play, try not to interfere or criticize. "Toddlers are less inhibited and less likely to censor themselves when they're acting a part," explains Dr. Erickson. Sometimes by playing dress-up, toddlers are trying to work out for themselves something they've seen or heard but don't quite understand. They may be trying out how it feels to be you and say some of the things you say, or they may be mimicking something they've picked up from a caregiver, sibling, or peer at preschool.

NOW THAT YOU KNOW

Dress for success. One of the fringe benefits of dress-up play for toddlers is that it helps them get better at seeing another person's point of view, says Dr. Harris. In fact, there is evidence that children who engage in a lot of role-play are better at empathizing with their peers than children who do not. Throw in the fact that kids who have strong empathy skills tend to be more popular with their peers, and you've got a pretty good argument for playing a little dress-up yourself.

Play along. If your toddler comes into the kitchen wearing her cape tomorrow morning, indulge the fantasy and address her as the person she is pretending to be. By acknowledging the character your toddler is playing, you boost her confidence. You also give her the chance to think about how another person—in this case, the dress-up character—thinks and feels. Don't be surprised if your child doesn't have the same preferences as Wonder Woman that she does as herself. As toddlers get older, they can create very elaborate characters, but even children who are still hovering around two can delight in the fun of pretending to be someone—or something—they're not.

Great imagination is for life. The benefits of a creative, well-developed ability to imagine do carry over into adult life. While many of us view imagination as a realm of childhood, Dr. Harris points out that an active one has countless practical applications in adult life, too. Through imagination, we are able to visualize things we hear described with language, consider what will happen next before we choose an action, and think about how other people will be impacted by the things we say and do. All of these skills based on the capacity for imagination in adults are just beginning to emerge in toddlers. For most, one of the primary ways they are learned is through fantasy play like dress-up.

Not just for Halloween. To help your toddler explore the fun of dress-up play, start a box of costumes and either take it out occasionally, or change its contents from time to time to keep the game fresh. Used Halloween costumes, hats of all kinds, and cast-off clothes and accessories from your closet all make wonderful additions to what will likely be a favorite play center for years to come.

Boys and girls will be girls and boys. Parents of toddlers sometimes get distressed to see a daughter determined to dress like Daddy or a son wearing a tiara in dress-up play. According to Dr. Erickson, what your child wears for play at this age has absolutely no bearing on his or her sexual orientation as an adult. At this age, children are exploring everything, including all kinds of roles. Gender identity is only a very small factor—or not a factor at all—in the roles they choose.

Chapter 3

WHY DO TODDLERS LOVE
TO PLAY OUTSIDE?

There are times when the effect of the great outdoors on a toddler seems nothing less than magical. Suddenly, the whiny are content, the bored are engaged, the tantrum is over, the child who can't seem to take a single step without you in the house is happy to go off and entertain himself in sand, leaves, grass, and playground toys.

No one knows precisely why spending time in a natural setting has a calming, healing, positive effect on people, but there is no doubt that it does. Studies have been conducted on the effects of exposure to fresh air, sunlight, and plant life on children, adults, and on patients recovering from surgery and illness. In each case, a natural environment provides benefits ranging from lowered stress and a more positive outlook to a lower heart rate and speedier recovery.

For toddlers, being outdoors opens up endless new avenues for exploring and experiencing unfamiliar sensations, all in an environment where they have a lot more latitude in their behavior than they do inside. Toddlers thrive in environments where they can be a little louder and a lot less physically confined. When you are one, two, or three, there are distinct joys to be found in climbing, tumbling, and getting your hands dirty that are rarely had without consequence indoors. According to Jane Perry,

Ph.D., research coordinator at the Harold E. Jones Child Study Center at the University of California at Berkeley and the author of *Outdoor Play: Teaching Strategies with Young Children,* the outdoors is also a place where toddlers get their earliest tastes of self-determination. Outdoor settings are places where children independently orchestrate their own relationships with the physical and social environment.

The less tangible effects on toddlers of discovering that the grown-ups are put at ease outside are valuable, too. "When the people around a toddler are relaxed in the company of a cool breeze, the shade of a willow, or the sweet smell of grass, the toddler is more inclined to relax, as well," says Dr. Perry.

All toddlers need outdoor play, and they flourish in it because at this stage of development, mastering their physical capabilities is a huge part of what they're destined to do. "Children need physical activity and the stimulation of full body movement in ways that only the expansiveness of outside can give," Dr. Perry points out. In addition to the immediate physical benefits, being outdoors stimulates brain development.

"Much of what the toddler is keenest about learning is how the world works," says Dr. Perry. "Small children are burgeoning scientists, always thinking, 'If I do this, what will happen?' The outdoors provides all kinds of hands-on experience, from the physics of gravity as water flows, a ball is tossed, or a body spins, to what animals look like and how plants grow."

NOW THAT YOU KNOW

Location, location, location. For some adults, outdoor play begins and ends on cleared land punctuated by playground equipment. Playground play is a great opportunity for your toddler, but try to expand his horizons to include more natural settings, too—a running stream, a hill to climb, sand and a shovel at the beach, and opportunities to observe wildlife are priceless experiences for toddlers.

Know the tools of the trade. If you're choosing outdoor play equipment, look for toys that incorporate natural materials, either in their construction or in their use (like toys that contain sand or water). Try to choose outdoor toys your toddler can use without your help so he can fully capitalize on the opportunity to play independently. "Some of the best equipment is homemade or readily available," says Dr. Perry, "[like] a big box for climbing in and out of, a grassy hill, and sand, sand, and more sand."

Get in touch with your toddler's social butterfly. Sometimes toddlers who find it hard to play with other kids will finally be able to break the ice outside. Making friends in a relaxed, wide-open atmosphere seems to be easier. Provide your toddler and her friends with opportunities to play that will let them make eye contact with one another. A round sandbox, a small pool, or a big bucket of leaves all make ideal settings for toddlers to make first overtures to other kids.

Wheels for beginners. Dr. Perry mentions that parents choosing outdoor toys for toddlers should go with a tricycle, and not a low-to-the-ground two wheeled bicycle with training wheels. Little bikes have gained a lot of popularity in recent years and come featuring some snazzy designs and cartoon characters, but low rider tricycles (like Big Wheels) give toddlers better physical stimulation because it takes a toddler's full body effort to propel them, rather than a concentrated effort from their legs.

A change of scene. Moving outdoors is sometimes a simple solution to the very perplexing problem of a toddler who is on the verge of a tantrum or in a miserable mood. Toddlers sometimes seem to get "stuck" in a mood or attitude, and it can take a move as dramatic as going from playroom to park to help them shake it off. "Young children are very often ready for the relief of a distraction from their stuck place," says Dr. Perry, "and what better full body distraction could there be than the multi-sensory change in scene from inside to outside?"

A familiar place. One of the ways toddlers learn about the natural world is by viewing and interacting with the same scene from day to day, month to month, and season to season. If you visit one or two outdoor spaces regularly, your toddler will begin to get a sense of his own place in that environment, and of how it changes while he is not there. It's an early exposure to the lessons of ecology, and it can give your toddler a wonderful foundation for an understanding and respect for nature later in life.

Chapter 4

WHY DO TODDLERS LOVE TO PLAY HIDE-AND-SEEK?

It all started with a game of peek-a-boo. You covered your face with a blanket, and your months-old baby knew you were still there and pulled it away. Just like that, the hide-and-seek years had begun.

With widely varying degrees of sophistication, toddlers relish their experiences with hiding and finding. They love to cover their eyes with their fat little hands and count haphazardly ("Two, three, four, nine, eight!") before they start seeking. They crouch down in their favorite hiding spot and wait no more than a minute before jumping out to shout "Here I am!" They thrive on the jolt of surprise that comes when they manage to discover you—beaming when they hear the much-anticipated "You found me."

Hide-and-seek is one of the rare gems of a game that really does grow with your child. At first, they're delighted to discover that objects (and people) that go out of sight haven't disappeared forever. As they get older and smarter, they determine that they can take the initiative and go find those missing things on their own. Toddlers at different ages have vastly different levels of understanding of the game, but even before they can play it with finesse, they love it.

The reason for toddlers' affection for hide-and-seek is one of nature's great provisions for growing children. "Toddlers enjoy the games that help them work on their developing cognitive and social skills. At this age, the activities they like best are the ones they learn the most from," explains Mark Strauss, Ph.D., a developmental psychologist and director of the University of Pittsburgh's Infant and Toddler Development Center. Hide-and-seek helps develop so many different skills, it holds children's interest for years.

Three of those skills are your child's burgeoning sense of his place in his surroundings, an increasingly sophisticated understanding of object permanence (the idea that a missing thing still exists in the world), and the very novel idea to a toddler that other people have thoughts unlike his own.

As adults, we subconsciously make spatial maps of everything we see, explains Dr. Strauss. We observe that the sofa is along the wall, the table is next to the sofa, the chair is in the corner, and so on, but toddlers are just beginning to learn to do this. Hide-and-seek encourages them to pay attention to spatial information, often really thinking about it for the first time.

Searching for hidden people and objects lets children take the idea of getting a handle on their environments one step further. In order to figure out where something has gone, they have to be able to imagine what happens to it while it's out of their sight. Imagining that people and things are moving and changing while they're not looking is a new and surprising idea for most toddlers, who truly believe that the world is what they see.

By imagining that people are busy hiding while she is counting, your toddler makes a big leap in the social skills department. "Toddlers are completely egocentric," explains Lisabeth DiLalla, Ph.D., a developmental psychologist at Southern Illinois University School of Medicine in Carbondale and director of SIU's Twins and Siblings Preschool Play Lab. "Learning to hide from another person and to seek another person out is a lesson where the toddler begins (ever so barely) to have an understanding that someone else has a different perspective from her own."

NOW THAT YOU KNOW

Think of hide-and-seek as Geography 101. If you're one of those people who gets disoriented when you step into the mall, let alone in a strange new city, you have some idea of how helpful it is to be able to grasp your geographical place in the world. Playing hide-and-seek with your toddler won't necessarily make her a master navigator or map-reader as an adult, but it's a very good start. Latitude and longitude are way over a toddler's head, but playing hide-and-seek helps him learn about the location of his body relative to his surroundings, what makes up his immediate environment, and the ways he can navigate through his home. Those simple lessons set the stage for more advanced spatial awareness—the very useful kind that helps grown-ups read road maps and find their lost cars in parking lots.

Take it one step further. Hide-and-seek is a great geographical experience on its own, but if you want to augment your child's learning on the subject, try helping your toddler make a map of your home and showing them how to follow it to an object. Another alternative is to turn hide-and-seek into a game of hints à la *Blue's Clues*. Let your child find picture clues to lead them through the house to a hidden object, and you may soon have a budding cartographer on your hands.

Stuffed Pooh likes to hide, too. There are countless variations on the game, and one of them is hiding objects that fit in places smaller than even those that can conceal a toddler. Playing hide-and-seek with toys is just as much a learning experience as playing with other people, and it opens a ton of new possibilities for the game, explains Dr. DiLalla. "Toddlers are wired to enjoy novelty," Dr. DiLalla says. "It's one of the major reasons they are such effective explorers of their worlds." Toddlers' interest in things that disappear and reappear actually helps develop their still-immature brains. Each time a toddler encounters something new, it allows new pathways, called synapses, to open in his brain so he can process what he has just experienced. This is the main way toddlers learn, so don't hesitate to come up with as many novel hiding-and-finding scenarios as you can.

Over, under, next to, and on. Hide-and-seek offers the perfect opportunity to teach your toddler words about where things are in relation to one another. By simply keeping a running commentary on a game ("Is Connor *under* the table? Nope. How about *behind* the door?") you give your toddler an insight into the use of all the positional words he's going to be trying to use on his own very soon.

Get physical. Toddlers learn tremendous amounts about themselves and the world through physical activity. Hide-and-seek is a great jumping off point to encourage your toddler to explore her body's presence. Give your toddler cardboard boxes to use for hiding spaces, help her hide in the bathtub, a laundry basket or any other safe place that makes her think about the way she physically fits (or doesn't fit!) into her surroundings.

Chapter 5

WHY DO TODDLERS LIKE TO READ THE SAME BOOKS OVER AND OVER AGAIN?

How many ways can most parents of toddlers read *Green Eggs and Ham*? We can read it in a boat. We can read it with a goat. We can read it in the rain, and in the dark, and on a train. We can even read it without peeking at the pages—because we've recited it dozens of times to our delighted toddlers, and we know it by heart.

Every mom loves to see her child take an early interest in books, and every dad envisions a future full scholarship when his first-born comes squirming onto his lap saying, "Read, Daddy." But when parents discover that most toddlers immediately follow "The End" with "Again!" they begin to wonder if one can really build a scholarship-quality mind on a steady diet of *Is Your Mama a Llama?*, *Brown Bear, Brown Bear*, and *Goodnight Moon*.

It turns out, most early literacy experts agree, that you can. Toddlers love to hear the same books over and over for very good reasons—both personal and developmental, explains Lisabeth DiLalla, a developmental psychologist at Southern Illinois University School of Medicine in Carbondale and director of SIU's Twins and Siblings Preschool Play Lab.

"Reading to your child is one of the most important things you can do to help her develop to her highest potential," Dr. DiLalla explains.

"Reading at all to your child does several critical things: it ensures a special time between the parent and child, it teaches children about the sequencing of events—that stories have a beginning, middle, and end—and it shows children that they can enjoy books." And though the research is not definitive, reading to your toddler may well help him to learn to read earlier as well.

Reading the same books again and again has even more benefits for toddlers than reading different books less often. Because the world of books is very new to the pre-pre-school set, re-reading gives them a chance to familiarize themselves with how stories are told, to learn all the words in a particular book (but only one or two new ones on each pass through it), and to start making connections between the illustrations they see and the story they hear at the same time.

Those connections take time to make, explains Mary Hynes-Berry, Ph.D., a professor at the Erikson Institute for Early Childhood in Chicago and professional storyteller, and that's where re-reading comes in. At approximately the same time that you are sick and tired of reading a particular book, chances are your toddler is just starting to feel confident with it. He's getting to the point where he can anticipate what's going to be on the next page, and sometimes even know the next word. "You can feel and see the anticipation building in a toddler who knows a favorite page is coming up next." Dr. Hynes-Berry smiles. "There's great satisfaction for them in knowing that something is coming and that they 'get it.' It's a huge confidence builder."

NOW THAT YOU KNOW

Read it again, and again. Though you may feel a bit like escaping to the jungles of your own room after reading *Where the Wild Things Are* for the third time on any given day, indulge your toddler in reading it one more time. The long-term paybacks can be enormous. Study after study has shown that kids whose parents regularly make time to read with them in the first three years of their lives do better in school than those who haven't been read to. As Dr. DiLalla explains, "Not all children who are read to will get all A's in school, but reading to your toddler will certainly help her to do the best she can." In fact, research has found that the amount of experience kindergarteners have with books in their preschool years is the best predictor of their reading comprehension all the way through elementary school.

Stop and talk about the flowers, the monsters, and the teddy bears. As long as you're going to be reading *Are You My Mother?* ad nauseum, you might as well get the most bang for your buck. Talking with your child while you read—whether you're asking him questions or pointing out pictures—is the best way to help him learn how to think about what he hears and sees in books. "You can start with pointing out specific objects or asking your child 'What color?' or 'How many?'" says Dr. Hynes-Berry. "And as your child learns to participate, you can ask them questions that let them make inferences, like 'How do you think that boy feels?' and 'What makes you think that?' Expert readers are always interacting with the text," she explains, "and talking about what you are reading with your toddler is a wonderful way to develop his ability to comprehend the written word."

Follow along with your finger. It may seem silly to underline the words you're reading for a child who is years away from reading independently, but research suggests that toddlers start to get a sense of how we read—left to right and top to bottom—by being guided through the text. Even as young as three, some children start recognizing words that have been pointed out to them.

Broaden the bookshelf. If you're sick and tired of reading the same book (Dr. Seussitis is the medical term) and feel compelled to broaden your toddler's horizons, show your son or daughter how much *you* like a favorite book and see if they follow suit. Toddlers are natural mimics, and if they see and hear you having a ball reading a book aloud, they may well decide that they, too, like that book best.

Look for a unique appeal. Many times the books a small child chooses can give parents insight into what's on their toddler's mind. Dr. Hynes-Berry says a child with temper issues may want to hear *Where the Wild Things Are* again and again, because it offers a steady flow of reassurance that it's okay to get mad. Or if you have a budding artist, you may notice your toddler is drawn to the books with her favorite illustrations—even the ones that have no words at all. If your child is fixed on one book, look for clues as to what the unique appeal of that book might be. For many, a book that deals with an emotion a toddler can't quite get a handle on—fear or jealousy, for example—may strike a chord. If so, sometimes just re-reading a book that deals with that emotion can help them work through it.

Make it fun. It's not too hard with material like *Mr. Brown Can Moo, Can You?* to make reading fun for toddlers. They love your voice, they love to play with you, and they love to have your undivided attention. If you can engage children in reading in a way that makes it fun for them—by changing your voice for different characters; encouraging your toddler to huff and puff like the big, bad wolf; or throwing a red dish towel over your head when you're channeling Little Red Riding Hood—then they'll learn the most important lesson about reading that you can offer: they'll learn to want to do it themselves.

Chapter 6

WHY DO TODDLERS PLAY NEXT TO, BUT NOT WITH, ONE ANOTHER?

You go to all the trouble to arrange a play date for your eighteen-month-old, figuring it's time to jumpstart his social life. Toddler Number Two arrives, and the two of them proceed to ignore one another, with the exception of a few sidelong glances, for an hour and a half. Did you make coffee and Rice Crispy treats for *this*?

It may seem like your date was a bust, but the whole idea of "play" with someone who is not Mom or Dad is still very new to toddlers—at least those who don't have older siblings. The chance to play next to one of his peers is the best and easiest way to get him started on the road to a social life of his very own. Some parents can't imagine why their toddlers might need such a thing, but there's a world of important social lessons waiting for your toddler that he'll never get from playing with just you. Playing *beside* another child almost always precedes playing *with,* so you've helped your little one take the first step toward friendship with this date—even if the giggling, sharing, and game-playing you were waiting for never happened.

The reason toddlers, especially younger ones, get together with what seems like a marked disinterest in one another is not that they don't want to play—it's that they haven't got the vaguest idea what it takes to interact together. They're still learning the rules about eye contact, social distance, friendly (and unfriendly) gestures, and language that will make it possible for them to one day engage in something as sophisticated as an actual game.

"Think about the way a mother plays ball with her toddler," explains Jo Ellen Vespo, Ph.D., a professor of psychology and child life at Utica College in New York. "The mother rolls the ball back and forth with the toddler, and when the toddler gets distracted, the mother knows how to get the toddler involved in the game again. Toddlers don't know how to do that for each other. At this age, you see the beginning of a preference to play with other children, but no practical skills to do so."

Step one in learning to play with other children is proximity. Ideally, this happens at a time when both toddlers are fed, rested, and cheerful enough to enjoy themselves. In the beginning, they engage in what child psychologists call "parallel play"—side by side, but not together. As their interest in one another heightens, you'll notice that they spend more time checking each other out. Watch closely and you'll see that toddlers who seem oblivious to their companions often imitate their actions.

Before long, those two kids will be yanking toys from each other's hands. After that, the trading phase will start. One day soon, they'll be cooperating to create their very own game. Each step brings your toddler a little bit closer to learning how to engage his peers, and to reaping the benefits of first friendships.

NOW THAT YOU KNOW

Parallel comfort zone. Some toddlers linger in the parallel play stage for much longer than others, moving on to a role that is more one of an observer than an equal participant. Don't worry if your toddler does this—it's very common for children with shy temperaments and kids who need a little extra time to adjust to other changes in their lives.

Studies show that a two-year-old wallflower is not necessarily destined to be one for life. Although children who are born with shy, reserved temperaments often carry those outlooks well into later childhood, many learn to overcome it over time.

Bring in a big kid. If you want to arrange a play date with benefits that seem a little more immediate for your toddler, set it up with a child who is a year or two older. By the age of three, and more so at four, explains Dr. Vespo, most toddlers have taken remarkable strides in their ability to play cooperatively. They're beginning to peacefully exchange toys and take turns, and they're beginning to be able to engage in fantasy play with other children ("You be the tiger, and I'll be the lion"). These socially advanced kids can help make your toddler's transition from observer to player a smooth one.

Host at home. If your toddler is having a hard time relaxing in the presence of other toddlers, there's no reason to push the issue. Take a break for a couple weeks, and arrange the next play date at your own house. Having the home turf can make the whole process less stressful for shy children, explains Dr. Vespo.

This kid again? Research has shown that multiple play dates with a single playmate usually help toddlers get a handle on their social skills more quickly and easily than play dates with a number of different friends. Even though you're not seeing much interaction between your toddler and her playmate at first, chances are the two children are getting more comfortable with each visit—and soon they'll be confident enough to extend a toy, a snack, or an invitation to play together with that familiar friend.

Of course, just like grown-ups, sometimes two toddlers really don't like one another. If your toddler doesn't get along with the child he's been spending time with, try another playmate to see if things go better.

Same time, same place. Letting your toddler get together with friends in a regular play space can help advance cooperative play. "Toddlers need practice with play routines in familiar play spots," says Jane Perry, Ph.D., research coordinator at the Harold E. Jones Child Study Center at the University of California at Berkeley. "Certain play places encourage social interactions because they are a regular and familiar feature of the child's play. Children this age are beginning to remember the last time, and the time before that, when they played in a spot. Their memory is just as much a part of the features of the play spot as the climbing structure or the sand."

What kind of game is best? If it's one that is hands-on, open-ended, and easily lends itself to working together, it might be a good choice for early play dates. Playing in a sandbox or at a sand table, or with a variety of dress-up clothes, for example, has plenty of room for two to work together or apart. A toy that takes two, like a big ball, works well, too.

Chapter 7

WHY DO TODDLERS ALWAYS WANT WHAT THE NEXT CHILD HAS?

Almost all toddlers go through a phase where they want nothing more nor less than what the next kid has—and one of the dirty little secrets of raising them is that the vast majority are not above pushing, pulling, hitting, and/or biting to get it. Most of us stew about our toddlers' "antisocial" behavior, wondering where we went wrong to be raising this little barbarian instead of a kid with a healthy understanding of "please" and "thank you."

If you're in this boat with your toddler right now, relax. The other mothers may be horrified when your toddler shoves and snatches to get what he wants, but they've all either been in your shoes already—or their turn is coming soon. There is nothing more normal than a little greedy, grabby play during the toddler stage.

"Toddlers' social skills are very, very raw," explains Tovah Klein, Ph.D., director of the Barnard Center for Toddler Development of Barnard College. "They don't know how to offer an invitation to play, or how to engage another child in play. What's more, when they see something they want, they feel like they really need it, and right now.

"What usually happens is that toddlers progress from parallel play to grabbing, pulling, and pushing. Adults think it's malicious, but for children this age, it's really just a way of saying, 'Hey! Notice me!'"

They do get noticed. If your toddler stages an attack on a younger toddler, she's going to hear about it in the form of screams and tears at the indignity of the encroachment. If she infringes on the territory of a child closer to her own stage of development, she may be on the receiving end of the same brutality almost immediately.

Parents' reactions to this kind of behavior are wide-ranging. Some make a quick decision that their toddlers need to be isolated from other kids until they've worked out their "aggression issues." Unfortunately, to work past this basest method of getting another child's attention, toddlers need a chance to learn from experience. Other parents overreact by spanking or making their child feel ashamed. This, too, doesn't work, because it'll make your toddler miserable for doing something in which he intended no harm.

"In a way, in this case you want your child to be a bully, not a wimp," Dr. Klein continues. "In order to move on to the next level of interaction, they have to have a sense of themselves."

Instead of going to either extreme in your reaction to a bullying moment from your toddler, get down to eye level with her and firmly say, "We do not hit" (or grab, or push). Then use those first awkward battles over toys as opportunities to show your toddler her new friends have wants and needs of their own. "By explaining to your child that this other person also wants that toy and is upset about it, you'll help her begin to realize other people have feelings, too," Dr. Klein explains. Say something like, 'Look, your friend is very sad. He wants to play with this, too.' Studies have shown children as young as 6 months are capable of paying attention to and responding to other people's emotions. Your toddler undoubtedly can do it, too. Helping your child to begin feeling empathy toward others will go a long way in helping her to make friends—and in learning, in the long run, to share toys.

NOW THAT YOU KNOW

Play dates, not play groups. "Play groups tend to be disastrous for toddlers," says Dr. Klein. Too many children and not enough social skills to go around can quickly lead to chaos and tears. Instead of trying to assemble five or six toddlers to play together, try only two.

Take it outside. Outdoor play tends to be more open-ended, less centered on toys, and easier for toddlers to enjoy peacefully. Part of the benefit may be because toddlers tend to spend their outdoor time more focused on play that tests their burgeoning large motor skills, and they can run, climb, skip, and jump on the playground without having to duke it out over any toys at all.

Put away the favorites. If you're going to host toddlers playing together, go ahead and put away your child's favorite toys ahead of time. Seeing her prized stuffed bear in the arms of another child may be enough to ruin a play date for a toddler who is just learning how to interact with others.

What's a "turn" anyway? Don't expect your toddler to understand what it means to "wait your turn." The concept is beyond their mental capacity in more ways than one. To get around that fact, Jo Ellen Vespo, Ph.D., professor of psychology and child life at Utica College, recommends introducing turn taking in a very concrete way, by means of an egg timer or kitchen timer. "If toddlers can actually see the time passing and hear it when a turn is over, they can begin to have some concept of what a 'turn' is and how it passes from one child to the next."

Take two, they're small. If you have any toys with exact or similar duplicates, start your play date out with those. Research has been done on whether toddler play goes more smoothly when there's more than one of a particular toy available, and it inevitably does. There will be occasions when the red ball the other kid has still seems somehow better and more desirable than the one yours is holding, but more often than not, duplicates can ease relations between toddlers who are trying their best to make friends.

Time is on your side. The "bully stage" of childhood play passes all on its own for most kids. "By age three, cooperative play usually starts to emerge, in an almost magical way," says Dr. Klein. So even if your own pronouncements about the reasons not to hit and push to get another child's toys are falling on deaf ears, your child is highly likely to figure out a better way for himself—and soon.

Chapter 8

WHY DO TODDLERS ALWAYS REPEAT THE WORST THINGS YOU SAY?

The last word you want to hear from your toddler is the one you say when you get cut off in traffic. Yet, inevitably, there it comes—high pitched, small voiced, but against all odds perfectly pronounced and spoken with sufficient emphasis that it's unmistakable. Later, when your precious toddler repeats the newly minted vocabulary word for your mother-in-law, the full impact of what you've done sinks in. No, your toddler has no idea what he's saying. Yes, now the whole world knows you swear like a sailor in front of him.

This almost universal experience among parents of toddlers is a case of a healthy toddler impulse gone bad, explains Stephanie Gottwald, MA, research coordinator at the Center for Reading and Language Research at Tufts University. Toddlers pick up most of their language skills by mimicking the people around them, she says—not just vocabulary, but pronunciation, word order, intonation, and even the emotional weight and social circumstances tied to specific words and phrases. It's a system that works in one form or another in most human societies. Unfortunately, it works a bit too well when it comes to curse words.

Under normal conditions, it takes young toddlers several repetitions of an expression to get down to picking out and repeating individual words. As they get older, they steadily get faster at grabbing out the new words. They hear phrases, sentences—a jumble of sounds that becomes clearer as they get a better handle on their language. Toddlers have to sift through a wealth of heard words to get to a single new one and try it out on their own.

Except, of course, for the ones we say all by themselves and deliver with feeling—"Hello!" "Uh-oh!" "Thank you" and "Damn it!" are among the chosen few. "Most nouns and verbs are so jumbled together with all the other words of a sentence that it's quite a feat that young children can pick them out at all," explains Gottwald. But curse words are often spoken more loudly and in a different pitch than the surrounding words (if, in fact, there are any other words to cushion the delivery). That makes them easy for little ears to pick out of a voice stream.

As if the fact that curse words jump into toddlers' waiting ears wasn't enough to inspire them to speak them on their own, the response they get when they do is almost always enough to keep them talking. Toddlers may be small, but they're not stupid. When they find that using a particular word gets a laugh out of Dad or their older siblings, or that they can throw Mom into a panic with it whenever they like, they'll use it for every circumstance from punctuating a fit to passing the time while you make dinner until they get good and tired of it.

NOW THAT YOU KNOW

Backtrack. As soon as the offending word is out of your mouth, before your toddler has had a chance to say it, replace it with another that's likely to catch those little ears. "Peanut butter!" "Scooby-Dooby-Doo!" "Sugar-booger!"—in short, anything that's going to sound more fun and interesting to your toddler than that other thing you just said. Now is not the time for muttering. Say your new replacement word with feeling. If you get it across fast enough, your tot won't have a chance to process your mistake into a usable word.

It's rhyme time. Damn it, bammit, slammit, glammit. There's more than one way to get out of getting caught swearing, but rhyming might be the best. By taking the offending word out of context and burying it in rhymes, you can take the emphasis off the word's meaning and put it on a silly sound. This method may seem like a means of deliberately confusing your toddler, but it is perfectly harmless and may even be beneficial. According to Gottwald, children who have frequently played rhyming games as toddlers will probably become better readers down the road than those who have not. Yes, that should make you feel better.

Turn the other ear. If your toddler has already picked up a curse word and you're trying to exorcise it from his vocabulary, the first step is to go cold turkey on the attention for its delivery. Whether you find your toddler's voicing of a few choice words adorable or mortifying, don't give it the time of day. The less return your little sailor gets for his choice expressions, the faster they'll drop out of his vocabulary (or at least into the category of infrequently used phrases). Sadly, this method will only work if you can get your whole family to participate. If your toddler doesn't get a rise out of you but can still reduce his sister to fits of giggles for his linguistic efforts, he's going to keep doing it.

Once a sailor? If your toddler has picked up a few curse words by the age of two, don't despair, says Diane Beals, Ed.D., associate professor of education at the University of Tulsa. It doesn't necessarily mean you're saddled with a foul-mouthed child for the next decade and a half. There's no point in punishing a child this age for swearing, but in another year or two, you'll have all sorts of recourse available to discourage the use of forbidden terminology. Once your child gets to an age where just the thought of a day without Cartoon Network strikes fear in his heart, you'll be able to wean him off his curse words by responding to them with suitable penalties.

There are other words out there. On the bright side, once you've discovered how easy it is to "teach" your child curse words, you may find it easier to teach him words you'd like him to know. When offering up a new word for his use, using the same method will help your toddler grasp it faster. While it's not necessary to shout phrases like "Excuse me!" or "Mom's the best!" when you get aggravated in traffic, if you'd really like to hear your toddler adopt the phrase into his vocabulary, it's well worth a shot.

Chapter 9

WHY DO TODDLERS PLAY WITH THE BOX AND NOT THE GIFT?

It was Christmas, and we'd been getting ready for weeks. On the big morning, Santa delivered a baby doll, a walking, talking action figure, Barney puppets, and a battery-operated jeep. By noon, toys were scattered from one end of the house to the other, and the kids were deeply involved in a game of king/princess/castle in, under, and around the box that had delivered my new pots and pans. Granny had inadvertently provided *the* hit holiday gift of the season when she chose the toddler-sized box of cookware.

"Boxes are wonderfully open ended, literally and figuratively," explains Joan Brooks McLane, Ph.D., professor of child development at the Erikson Institute in Chicago, in trying to explain why toddlers often end up playing more enthusiastically with a gift's packaging than its contents. "There are so many different things you can do with them. They're fun to get in and out of, to hide things in, to decorate and to change. They can be one thing today and something entirely different tomorrow."

Therein lies the difference between a plain old box and the majority of toys on the market. A box is what you make it. "It can become a dollhouse, puppet stage, school, or an alien planet," points out Marian

Diamond, Ph.D., professor of integrative biology at the University of California at Berkeley and author of *Magic Trees of the Mind: How to Nurture Your Child's Intelligence, Creativity and Healthy Emotions from Birth Through Adolescence.* "When it comes to providing toys and activities for young children, there is often an inverse relationship between how specific and elaborate the toy is and how much it will excite a child's imagination."

While there are lots of great toys for toddlers on the market, there is truth to the suggestion that the things that make them attractive to the adults who shop for toys—elaborate design, instructive features, bright lights, colors, and audio features—can also mean that they have limited applications for a toddler who is constantly busy moving on to the next big thing.

"The thing that sometimes happens with a new and exciting-looking toy is that kids are really interested initially, but then run out of enthusiasm when they run out of things to do with it," says Dr. McLane.

A cardboard box, though it has no bells and whistles, offers all kinds of play potential. In addition to the unlimited possibilities for a toddler's imagination, it holds physical thrills. Getting into and out of a big box, covering up with it, tipping it on its side and using the flaps as doors all give toddlers new perspectives on their own size, strength, and how they fit into their surroundings. Seeing how they can and can't manipulate a new space is a delight out of all proportion to the simplicity of the container.

NOW THAT YOU KNOW

Today, the box; tomorrow, the toy. Just because your toddler wants to play with the box today and not the new toy doesn't mean that'll be the case tomorrow, next week, or next year. The time when parents are most acutely aware of their children's fascination with cardboard boxes often comes on occasions that bring not just one new toy, but lots. In the excitement of a party or a holiday, and faced with an abundance of toy riches, young children often retreat to something simple and unintimidating, like a box. If your toddler ignores his new toys on a special occasion, try reintroducing them at a rate of one or two a day over the next few days. Taken one thing at a time, chances are he'll be eager to play with his new loot.

Use it play-by-play. It doesn't take much effort to use your toddler's new favorite toy as a teaching tool. According to Dr. McLane, toddlers learn new concepts more easily when they experience both the words and the actions together, making interaction with a big box the next best thing to its own lesson plan. Here are just a few suggestions for making the most of yours:

- Help your toddler learn positional terms by keeping a running commentary on his physical relationship to the box: "And now, ladies and gentlemen, Brendan is *under* the box. But wait! Brendan is *next to* the box. Would you look at that? Brendan is *behind* the box." Your toddler will delight in being the center of attention, and he'll gain a better understanding of physical relationships in the process.

- Break out the paint or markers and teach your toddler the names of colors while you take turns decorating your treasure.

- Feed your toddler's creativity by showing him all the things just one box can be: on its side, a cave where he can pretend to be a bear; upright, your toddler can climb inside and be a present to be delivered to you (surprise!); upside down, with black circles drawn on top, it's a stove to cook on and play kitchen.

- Get your toddler thinking ahead, a skill that still requires a lot of effort from him, by asking him what he would need to take with him in his box if it were a spaceship, a boat, a school bus, a tractor, or an airplane. Let him tell you what he'd carry on for each kind of trip. You can even help him pack a bag and get on board.

If it works here . . . One of the best things parents can learn from watching what kids do with a plain box is to get a sense of what interests our toddlers and how we can create other opportunities to play together with them. If your toddler loves nothing better than to hide in his box, try making sheet-over-chair tents for him another day. If it turns out that decorating the box is what your child likes best, consider investing in an easel and paints for the budding artist. If your toddler instantly launches into dramatic play in the presence of his box—for example, growling like a tiger whenever he's inside—try playing puppets or dress-up with him. Come to think of it, that box you've got would make a nifty puppet theatre. . . .

Chapter 10

WHY DO TODDLERS LOVE TO RIDE, BOUNCE, SPIN, AND SWING?

You can sense your toddler's reckless joy when she spins round and round or does her best imitation of a run at top speed until she drops. Any adult who has ever played a pickup game of basketball, danced until dawn, or screamed through a roller-coaster ride can on some level appreciate what a small child takes away from those first, all-out, intense physical efforts. But when the athlete in question is your own child, whose safety is your personal mission in life, it can be terrifying. When you see her running, jumping, and spinning with abandon, you know a crash is inevitable. Our toddlers' physical explorations bring out the overprotective grandma in us all.

The reasons toddlers spin, swing, and race as if the world is their own private amusement park boil down to the fact that at this stage of development, both their bodies and their brains demand stimulation to develop. In this case, the input is physical, mental, sensory, and what's called vestibular stimulation—spurring the body's balance center in the inner ear.

As adults, we often take both our fine-tuned sense of balance and our fundamental understanding of our place in the spaces around us for granted. For toddlers, those abilities are still developing, becoming more complete and connected, one tumble, jump, swing, and spin at a time.

Studies dating back to the 1970s have shown that vestibular stimulation in infants hastens their motor development—infants who were spun in a chair while being held in different positions at Stanford University showed better motor development than their nonspun peers. The difference in this kind of stimulation for toddlers, of course, is that they don't need anyone to spin them. They're quite capable of doing it themselves.

Consider what happens to a toddler when she takes a turn on a swing. The child experiences up and down, back and forth, side to side, the importance of balance and grip, the dizzying visual input that comes with all that movement—all at once.

First-time parents often look at their toddlers as they race from activity to activity—demonstrating all the physical moves in their repertoire along the way—and wonder if they're raising a child with a hyperactivity problem. Rest assured that just because a toddler seems to have a manic streak during this stage does not mean she'll be racing that way for the rest of her life.

NOW THAT YOU KNOW

A time for every purpose. As important to your toddler's development as this kind of physical play is, it's fine to set some basic limitations on the times and places where it is allowed. Your toddler should have opportunities every day for physical and vestibular stimulation, says Jane Perry, Ph.D., research coordinator at the Harold E. Jones Child Study Center at the University of California at Berkeley and the author of *Outdoor Play: Teaching Strategies with Young Children.* At the end of the day, it will have been good for both of you.

Take a class. Your toddler may not need a bit of help getting the physical stimulation she needs, but if she's a bit reticent, or if you would like to enjoy more physical play with her and don't know how to initiate it, consider taking a class together. Programs like Kindermusik, Brain Gym, and Gymboree are partly based in research on the importance of vestibular stimulation, and their classes will give you lots of ideas for fun, enriching play with your toddler at home.

This kind of fun is not for everyone. If your toddler has decided that swinging or spinning is not for her, don't push the issue. While riding in the car is inevitable, a child who doesn't want to ride the playground equipment or twirl in Daddy's arms should never be forced. Some kids are extremely sensitive to vestibular stimulation and do not enjoy it (some adults are, too). Others find it oddly addictive. If your toddler is starting to show signs of being prone to motion sickness, she may limit her own exposure to the kinds of movement that make her feel ill.

A sign of other things. Most toddlers, given plenty of active playtime indoors and outside, seem to achieve the right amount of vestibular stimulation on their own. For a few, though, that balance is hard to reach. Toddlers who have physical or mental developmental delays may need a little help to get started in things like rolling, rocking, and getting a feel for up-and-down and side-to-side movements. As long as your toddler seems to be enjoying herself, you can push her on a swing, show her how to roll on a carpet, or help her rock on an oversized ball. By getting the ball rolling, both literally and figuratively, you can help facilitate balance and brain stimulation for a child who might not do so on her own.

Chapter 11

WHY DO TODDLERS ENDLESSLY ARRANGE AND REARRANGE THEIR TOYS?

If you give a toddler a box of toys, there are endless ways he can tackle it. Some will dump everything out and play with the box. Some will choose one toy and spend hours putting it through its paces. Some will set up an elaborate game of imagination, giving each object a distinctive voice and perspective.

Some will be what play researchers sometimes refer to as patterners. They will look at each toy in relation to all the others and try to sort out how that toy is similar, different, and relative.

If you give a patterner a box of plastic animals, chances are he'll start arranging them—by size, by color, by species, zoo animals over here, dinosaurs over there, sea animals in the sink, and so on. You may have to ask him to explain how a particular group of animals winds up together or arranged just so (and he may not be in the mood to explain it to you), but he will always have a reason.

"Part of playing for toddlers is exploring how things go together," explains Tovah Klein, Ph.D., director of the Barnard Center for Toddler Development of Barnard College in New York City. "They are learning how things are alike and not alike, learning that everything is relative."

In some cases, toddlers who are particularly adept at sorting, arranging, and classifying are giving their parents a glimpse of high intelligence to come. The ability to make connections and understand how one thing relates to the next at an early age is one of the established indicators of high IQ later in life.

A propensity for pattern play over imaginative play may also point to a specific kind of intelligence. Researchers at Harvard University, led by education professor and acclaimed author Howard Gardner, Ph.D., have been the leaders in a movement in the educational community to view intelligence in children (and adults) not by asking "How much?" but by inquiring "What kind?" Dr. Gardner came up with a theory of multiple areas of intelligence, based on the assumption that each person's mental capacity is made up of all of them, but that we each have areas of particular strength. The list includes linguistic, musical, bodily, mathematical/logical, spatial, naturalist, interpersonal and intrapersonal intelligences.

Toddlers who are fascinated with patterns, arrangements, and how things relate to one another—usually in a very visual way at this age—are showing you they have an especially solid capacity for logical intelligence. Lucky for you, children and adults with this area of strength often excel in their formal education, especially in math and science.

NOW THAT YOU KNOW

The all-purpose toddler. Regardless of what areas of intellectual strength you see in your toddler, this stage of his life is the one in which all types of intelligence should be cultivated and explored. If putting things into patterns seems to be a particularly effective way for your child to understand them, use that method as you expose him to other areas of strength: help him think about words that mean the same thing as one another; collect leaves or flowers together and organize them by size, shape, or color; or help him make a collage of photos of family members so he can start deciphering which cousins are connected to which aunts, uncles, and grandparents.

Give it a name. Toddlers often start categorizing their toys before they have a vocabulary extensive enough to put names to the groups they make. Talk with your child about the way he sets up his toys, and you'll enrich his vocabulary and his understanding of relationships by giving him the words he needs to label his groups by size, color, shape, and so on.

What else can you do with that? If your toddler is fascinated with discovering and playing out the patterns in his toys, get down on the floor with him and help him find some new ones. Most toddlers are thrilled when we share their enthusiasm for their toys, and you can almost see their little mental gears turning when you suggest lining up the Matchbox cars in an alternating color pattern, or seeing which of the balls in his collection will float in the bathtub. Don't push your toddler to play in ways that don't interest him, but do offer suggestions that will allow him to view his toys in new and different ways.

Chapter 12

WHY DO TODDLERS PUT THINGS IN THE VCR, DVD, TOILET, AND HEAT VENTS?

The ability of toddlers to devastate technological equipment may be one of the most frustrating aspects of parenting them—and one of the few issues for which waiting for them to grow out of it can be both infuriating and very, very expensive. Every toddler accidentally demolishes something, but some are impressive in their conquests. Consider Joey Taylor, one very bright, inquisitive, energetic little boy in upstate New York. In just the year he was two, Joey rendered two VCRs, a TV, a toaster oven, and an assortment of clocks and watches inoperable. He did some substantial damage to the refrigerator, too, but it soldiered on. Joey's methods generally involved either putting foreign parts in or taking necessary parts out. He was quite capable of destroying any piece of equipment in the amount of time it took his mom to make a cup of coffee—though he preferred to spend more time figuring out the workings of his victims. Though Joey never seemed to see it coming, he always felt terrible that he'd broken one more thing.

The bright side of all the destruction he created as a toddler is that when Joey got to kindergarten, his teacher informed his parents that he was extremely bright. Now in the third grade, he's a straight-A student in the gifted program at his school. Instead of breaking household appliances, he is beginning to try his hand at maintaining and repairing them. What once seemed like a curse on the harmony of Joey's family has turned into a blessing.

All toddlers touch things they are not supposed to touch, take things apart that are supposed to stay together, and experiment with how things fit—or don't fit—into one another, says Jo Ellen Vespo, Ph.D., professor of psychology and child life at Utica College. Curiosity is a natural, normal part of toddlerdom, and few children make it through the stage without breaking/spilling/losing something valuable—usually something they discovered because they saw it was a favorite of Mom or Dad.

As in the case of Joey Taylor, however, intense, never-ending, hope-he-doesn't-drop-that curiosity can also be an early indicator of high intelligence. Other common traits in gifted toddlers include an intense interest in figuring out cause and effect relationships, a high energy level, and the ability to come up with many different uses for toys and other objects—uses like prying the cover off the portable CD player with a pen, or using a Lincoln Log to prop open the door of the VCR.

Not every toddler who ruins a PC is going to grow up to be a genius, but most do learn from their early hands-on experiences with the plumbing, electronics, and mechanical equipment that keeps your house ticking. By all means, do what you can to minimize the damage, but when it seems like there's no end in sight to the vigilance it takes to get your toddler from breakfast to bedtime without anything getting broken, keep in mind that in just a few years, that same child may be the only one in your household who fully understands the current technology—and you're going to need him to help you learn how to use it.

NOW THAT YOU KNOW

Clear a path. You may think you've already sacrificed enough in the decorating department for your toddler, but putting big temptations out of harm's way for a couple years really is the best course of action if you want to keep electronics and other breakables functioning for the future. Some toddlers are dissuaded by gates and/or locks on cabinets, and some are not. Undoubtedly, by now you know which group your toddler belongs to. If you think any of the nontoy items amusing your toddler are potentially dangerous, go the extra mile to get it out of sight and mind. As hard as you try, you can't be watching all the time.

Jump on the bandwagon. If you have a toddler who is highly curious about the way things work, don't spend all your time telling her "don't." Highly inquisitive toddlers are often very bright ones, and you can feed their natural curiosity in a number of ways that won't hurt them or your stuff. If your toddler is fascinated with one particular piece of equipment, consider teaching her how to use it, supervised. After all, the toddler who knows exactly how to put a Barney disk in the DVD player and start it won't be as likely to insert a graham cracker.

Bigger, better toys. For some toddlers, the crux of the problem boils down to a lack of stimulation. If you think your toddler fits the description of an intellectually gifted child above, consider offering more sophisticated toys. Age labels on toy packaging are only guidelines, and if your toddler is bored with "Under 3" fare, supervise him playing with toys designed for an older child. Keep in mind, though, that a toddler who is a genius is some areas may very well still put things in his mouth that don't belong there, so be aware of small pieces as he plays.

Wasted warnings. Unfortunately, no number of warnings about the consequences of getting into the stereo or the laptop is enough to really stop your toddler from doing it anyway, explains Dr. Vespo. Toddlers are not yet capable of curbing their impulses enough to resist the temptations of toys they have their hearts set on. Their ability to remember is also still developing, and often not clear enough to recall something you told them *not* to do. Do tell your toddler if you expect him not to touch something—it will sink in over time—but don't think for a minute that that means he's going to be able to restrain himself.

Interrupt gently. If you have the type of toddler who feels the need to test, touch, and take apart everything in your house, don't be surprised if your "Honey, don't touch that" requests fall on deaf ears. Rest assured your child is not ignoring you for the sake of making you upset. Toddlers are very capable of becoming so engrossed in their explorations that they block out the sounds around them. In fact, deep concentration is another of the traits commonly found in gifted children. To redirect your child, gently touch him to get his attention, establish eye contact, then go from there.

Chapter 13

WHY ARE TODDLERS SO FASCINATED WITH BABIES?

"Baby!" For many toddlers, it's one of the first words, right up there with "dog," "kitty," "grandma," and "cookie." Babies in the grocery store, babies at family get-togethers, even a baby in Mommy's tummy provide an endless source of fascination for these little people who are only one step removed from being babies themselves.

Research has concluded that people do not have memories—at least not accessible memories—of their infancy. This is true of toddlers, who haven't had very long on their personal timelines to forget. Although they can't remember, toddlers do seem to have a good sense of the fact that they were babies in the not-too-distant past, says Megan McClelland, Ph.D., associate professor of human development and family sciences at Oregon State University. "They do know that there is a transition going on," Dr. McClelland explains, "that they were babies before, that they are working very hard not to be babies now."

Regardless of whether they coo and admire babies or coldly assess their faults, toddlers usually come around to reminding us of one important point when they take stock of their younger counterparts: "That's a baby. I am not a baby."

From the first time she says, "No," your toddler is bound and determined to separate herself from being a baby and get on with being a big kid—well, at least when the mood suits her. Oddly enough, many toddlers will regress before your very eyes in the presence of a baby—even while dishing about the baby's inferiority. Don't be surprised to see your toddler crawling, curling up in your lap, and sucking her thumb during or soon after a visit with a baby. Expect this behavior in spades if you have given what your toddler deems too much attention to the invading baby.

If the baby in question is just passing through, then chances are any feelings your toddler has about her will be transient, too. But when your family is welcoming a new baby, as your toddler forges a relationship with her new brother or sister, you can expect to see her love/hate relationship with both the real baby and her inner one dueling it out for weeks or even months.

NOW THAT YOU KNOW

If only you could bottle this confidence. You can delight your toddler and gently nudge her toward acting more maturely by helping her come up with all the ways she is bigger, stronger, and smarter than a baby. Babies have notoriously unbruisable feelings about these things, and toddlers love to brag.

Let her sort things out for herself. In the same way that toddlers explore issues that are on their minds when they play dress-up and make-believe, they sometimes work issues out for themselves by acting like babies. Don't punish or put down your toddler for playing at being a baby, but don't push her to do it, either. Sometimes parents have a hard time getting toddlers to wrap up the "baby game" at times when the behavior of a bigger kid is needed. If that's the case with your child, try offering an older-child's privilege, like a game of hide-and-seek or an opportunity to color or paint, if she'll cooperate. Give her "imaginary immaturity" the same space and respect you give her other games. Left to her own devices, she'll get tired of it when she's played the game out to her satisfaction.

A girl thing? Many toddlers of both sexes take an interest in babies, wanting to check them out, play with them, imitate them, and help take care of them. Between ages two and three, toddlers get a good feel for who they are and start to identify strongly with their same-sex role models, says Jo Ellen Vespo, Ph.D., professor of psychology and child life at Utica College. You may notice your daughter taking more of a shine toward babies at this time if her mom does. Likewise, if Dad makes a fuss about a baby, your toddler son may pick that up. Toddlers often imitate across gender, too, but don't be surprised to see your same-sex toddler trying to handle a baby the same way you do.

Just the two of us? No matter how amused and delighted your toddler may be with the baby in his life—whether that baby is a sibling, a cousin, or a stranger in a restaurant—don't leave them alone together for a second. The combination of toddlers' fickle nature—love it this minute, hate it the next—and their inability to fully understand the fragility of another person is a dangerous one for the baby. Your toddler might never intentionally hurt a baby, but you need to ensure it never happens accidentally.

Chapter 14

WHY DO TODDLERS HAVE IMAGINARY FRIENDS?

Contrary to the impression many of us have of lonely, introverted children dreaming up imaginary friends, research shows that most kids who invent make-believe companions are the sociable, outgoing kind. They are also resourceful: in the absence of real friends to play with, they create their own.

Researchers have demonstrated that children as young as eighteen months engage in pretend play; you've probably seen it at home—your toddler pretending to eat imaginary food or walk an imaginary pet. Amazingly, by the age of two-and-a-half, many children already have sophisticated enough imaginations to create pretend friends.

Toddlers who make up playmates are in very good company. It's hard to nail down the numbers for something as elusive as companions who don't actually exist, but it's been estimated that as many as 65 percent of children have them.

We really shouldn't be surprised to see our children inventing imaginary characters, explains Marjorie Taylor, Ph.D., professor of psychology at the University of Oregon in Eugene and author of *Imaginary Companions and the Children Who Create Them*. In a culture that exposes children to fantasy from their first days—in the form of everything from talking stuffed animals to cartoon characters to the Easter Bunny—kids are coached even before they can speak in the fun and excitement of believing in what they cannot see, smell, touch, and feel.

The reasons toddlers invent imaginary friends are diverse, but in most cases, they boil down to fulfilling an emotional need or desire. For some, imaginary companions are company in times of boredom or loneliness—one reason they're especially common among children who don't have siblings. For others, imaginary friends give confidence when a toddler is afraid, reassurance when they're intimidated—even someone to boss around when they're feeling powerless. Some imaginary friends are even "willing" to take the fall for their flesh-and-blood counterparts, turning up just at the moment a toddler thinks he needs someone to blame for breaking a dish or swiping a piece of candy.

The fringe benefit of imaginary friends is that they can help a toddler work through a range of issues from a safe distance—from frustration over toilet training to anger at Mommy and Daddy to his concern about a sick grandparent. When your toddler tells you her imaginary friend *hates* you, it's a way for her to express her anger without directly attacking you—an emotional safety net.

Dr. Taylor points out that the way some children use their imaginary friends has a lot of similarity to the form of therapy for adults to face their fears known as systematic desensitization. In the therapy, a patient begins by imagining the thing they fear, and works up to dealing with it in person. A child can go through a very similar process by subjecting her imaginary friends to her worst fears—and seeing how *they* fare against them.

Imaginary friends often change as a child's needs change, explains Dr. Taylor. A two-year-old may just be looking for a playmate; a four-year-old may be struggling to make sense of the dynamic at a new preschool; a six-year-old may need a place to vent anger towards her mom or her friends.

One of the big concerns parents have about imaginary friends is that they seem to loosen a toddler's grip on reality. Dr. Taylor's research and interviews with hundreds of children suggests that imaginary friends rarely overstep their bounds. "Children do become emotionally involved in their adventures with their imaginary friends," she explains, "but the experience is similar to what happens to an adult who becomes emotional while reading a novel or watching a movie—the emotions are real, but even if you are in tears, your grip on what is reality and what is fantasy is not compromised.

"Many times I have interviewed a child about an imaginary companion," Dr. Taylor continues, "and the child observes as I take notes. At some point in the interview, many children will lean over and look me in the eyes and remind me, 'You know, it's just pretend.'"

💡 Now That You Know

Your child's friend and you. As a parent, the real issue regarding imaginary friends is often what the adults are supposed to do with them. Some treat imaginary friends like sacred cows, evidence of their child's intelligence and creativity. Some ignore them, willing them to hurry up and go away. "Most children delight in having their parents play along," says Dr. Taylor, "but there's no reason to let yourself be manipulated by an imaginary child any more than you would allow from a real one." In short, as long as the imaginary friend doesn't interfere with the workings of your family or disregard the rules of your home, it doesn't hurt to join in.

Laying blame. The irritating thing about imaginary friends is sometimes that they are such little troublemakers. Someone ate all the cookies? Of course it was Ziggy. Someone broke Daddy's model airplane? Ziggy again. "Parents don't have to be concerned about stifling the friend," says Dr. Taylor. "In some cases you can sit down and talk with your child and explain that 'This is something we don't do, and we're going to help Ziggy learn not to do it, too.'" If a problem persists, though, try treating the situation the same way you'd treat it if your toddler was blaming a sibling or a real friend. A simple, "I know Ziggy didn't make this mess. Let's clean it up," should be enough at this age to get the idea across that you're not letting the imaginary friend be your toddler's fall guy.

Friends for life? As a general rule, most of us think of imaginary friends as creatures of toddlers and preschoolers. According to Dr. Taylor, however, they can hang around for as brief a period as a few days, or as long as several years. As children mature, they tend to keep their imaginary friends more to themselves—so much so that many parents don't realize they're still there.

Imaginary friends have rules, too. Perhaps the most distressing thing about your toddler's imaginary friends is that they may sometimes say or do things that make your child upset. Some friends! If your toddler begins to act afraid or distressed by something an imaginary companion is doing, the most effective way to handle it is often to play along and "discipline" the make-believe character in the same way you would your own child. "Now, Casper, if you're going to play in our house, you'll have to follow our rules. We do not yell at each other here," or something similar should do the trick—and may have your toddler in stitches, too.

Reality check. "While children with real emotional problems often have imaginary companions, having an imaginary companion does not mean that the child has problems," says Dr. Taylor. As long as your toddler seems to be healthy and well-adjusted in the "real" world of his life, there's no reason to believe the existence of an imaginary companion is problematic. If the imaginary friend is just one issue for a toddler who seems to be struggling in other areas, or if the imaginary friend seems to really be upsetting your toddler, share the situation with your family's pediatrician and ask for his or her opinion.

part two

Mealtime Mayhem

Chapter 15

WHY DO TODDLERS REFUSE TO EAT ONE DAY AND EAT EVERYTHING IN SIGHT THE NEXT?

Every parent of a toddler has seen it. One day, this child inhales food like she's just been rescued from a deserted island. We wonder if maybe we should intervene, because it seems like two pounds of macaroni in a twenty-eight-pound toddler is way too much. The next day, the same toddler subsists on a banana and two cups of milk—usually with us begging her to eat something more from breakfast until bedtime.

Why can't toddlers eat like normal people?

The fact is that toddlers have it all over "normal" people when it comes to eating habits. Instead of consuming meals at scheduled intervals, they eat when their bodies need the calories—and if left to their own devices, they won't eat when they've already taken in enough.

In observing and testing the eating patterns of toddlers, Jennifer Fisher, Ph.D., assistant professor of pediatrics and nutrition at Baylor College of Medicine, points out that research finds most toddlers consume a pretty steady number of calories in an average day. In fact, studies have found that toddlers who eat foods that appear the same but are unequal in calories (like low fat yogurt versus regular yogurt) make up for the differences in their next meal—with the kids who took in fewer calories eating more. These toddlers are not reading labels; they're just very in tune with their bodies' nutritional requirements. Though their intakes vary wildly from one meal to the next, things usually balance out over a twenty-four-hour period. If you string together several of those twenty-four-hour periods, you'll often find a surprisingly well-balanced diet, at least in terms of numbers of calories.

Of course, all calories are not created equal. Your toddler would probably be very happy to take in his full day's allotment in the form of chocolate ice cream if you'd let him. He may already occasionally blow most of his calories on fruit juice.

"Kids prefer flavors associated with high levels of energy (lots of calories), including foods that are sweet and high in fat," explains Dr. Fisher. Adults generally share the same preferences, because those tastes are deeply rooted and instinctive. The desire for high calories and high fat would be a handy means of perpetuating our species in a world of limited food supply, but in an environment where food comes in an abundance of high fat, sugar-saturated forms, it can lead to diets that are full of empty calories.

The trick for parents, explains Dr. Fisher, is not to ensure that our toddlers clean their plates or eat a certain weight of one or another food each day, but to make sure they are selecting their foods from healthy, nutritionally worthwhile choices. For example, if you offer your toddler a plate with a quarter cup of blueberries, a slice of whole wheat bread, a scrambled egg, a few bites of any vegetable and a cup of milk, there *are* no poor choices. Whatever your toddler eats will provide nutritious calories and allow her to maintain the healthy habit of eating only as much as she needs to not feel hungry.

If you're worried that a toddler who only takes a few nibbles from the plate described above might not be getting enough food to thrive, consider that that plate, along with three whole-grain crackers with peanut butter, half a banana, and one more glass of milk, meets most toddlers' nutritional requirements for an entire day. Sometimes in our enthusiasm for seeing our children flourish, we forget that the right-sized portions for them are just a fraction of the size of our own.

NOW THAT YOU KNOW

Are you hungry, honey? Most of us were raised to believe in the importance of cleaning our plates, and in the social consequences of taking
too long or not long enough with our meals. There's nothing wrong
with social graces, but they shouldn't be substituted for healthy eating
habits. Dr. Fisher says studies show that those toddlers with parents
who emphasize things like time length left in a meal, or the amount of
food on the plate—instead of focusing on whether the child was hungry—were less capable of regulating their own caloric intake than their
peers. Instilling healthy eating habits in toddlers for the long term
means respecting their own assessments of whether they're hungry or
full—even when there's still food on the plate.

The idea of letting their children eat (or not eat) at will worries
some parents to no end, but research done at Pennsylvania State University has clearly shown that the more controlling parents are of their
children's eating habits, the less healthy those eating habits become.
Someday your precious toddler is going to be making decisions about
food all alone, and a solid ability to regulate her own diet is the best
preparation you can give her.

Little bodies, little bellies. Sometimes as parents we start to worry our toddlers just can't be getting enough to eat. If your toddler is growing at a
normal rate, you probably have nothing to worry about. But if it's driving
you crazy, try writing down everything your child eats for a few days. How
much is enough? Over the course of a full day, just two ounces of protein,
two cups of milk, half of one orange, four tablespoons of peas, and two
slices of whole wheat bread will pretty much cover it. Chances are, when
you see your toddler's intake on paper, you'll discover that it's enough.

No bargaining zone. It's far too easy to get even the smallest child to
choke down her vegetables with a bribe of dessert. Unfortunately, research into young children's eating habits suggests that by doing so we

slide vegetables to the "don't like" foods list—possibly forever—and further glorify the attributes of anything labeled "dessert." Encourage your child to try new foods and to eat her fruit and veggies, but don't dangle that chocolate chip cookie to do so. In the long run, she'll have a higher regard for healthy fare because of it.

Practice what you preach. Dr. Fisher's research has clearly demonstrated that children whose parents actually eat the foods they'd like their toddlers to eat have healthier diets than those whose parents are all talk. Your toddler is paying close attention to your actions, and modeling many of them to a T. Telling your toddler to drink her milk while you down a Dr. Pepper sends mixed signals. Try to keep in mind that the single biggest factor in what a toddler eats is what foods are available in his home.

Chapter 16

WHY DO TODDLERS INSIST ON EATING ONLY ONE (OR TWO) FOODS DAY AFTER DAY?

Most parents of toddlers have to sit down on one occasion or another and ask themselves that critical question: Can my child really survive on only bananas? (or peanut butter? or macaroni? or pickles?) The eating habits of toddlers are erratic at best, but when your picky eater suddenly decides that nothing except pizza crust shall ever pass into his mouth again, the dull worry about your child's nutrition can turn into full-blown alarm.

There are many reasons children reduce their food intake when they hit the toddler phase—often by deciding there are only a few items they're willing to eat. One of those is toddlers' discovery that they do have a choice. The whole experience of expressing their own likes and dislikes gives toddlers a new avenue to start feeling independent. Many play that newfound independence to the hilt by deciding that pretty much any food that's someone else's idea is unacceptable, regardless of how it tastes. "No" becomes the word-of-the-month around this time, and it gets plenty of use at the table.

There's much more at work in toddlers' picky eating habits, though, than attitude. "Mother Nature puts the brakes on toddlers' eating because their rate of growth needs to slow down," explains Harriet Worobey, MA, director of the Nutritional Sciences Preschool at Rutgers

University. "They certainly can't continue to get bigger at the rate they experience in their first year. They've undergone a tremendous growth spurt, but now it's time to grow more slowly and start getting some exercise." The result is little bodies, now upright, that start to become longer and leaner, outgrowing their former butterball selves.

Coming right in line with the power struggle at the table is another interesting instinct that kicks in. Toddlers—once infants who would happily eat literally anything—start thinking twice about putting new things in their mouths. This often comes across as pickiness to parents, but in fact, nature provides toddlers with what scientists term neophobia—a fear of new things—to help them survive their first independent forays into the world. In laboratory studies, infants will put anything in their mouths—even potentially poisonous substances and things that adults would find repulsive (all simulated for the study, of course). Young toddlers, though, hesitate at things like bugs, garbage, and chemicals. This new instinct to be cautious of new things usually begins just about the time babies become capable of getting up and walking and lingers until toddlers begin to look and act more like "big kids"—around age four. Unfortunately, the new defense often extends beyond dish liquid and dog fur to foreign substances like meatloaf, broccoli, and kiwi.

If all the factors that prevent toddlers from branching out in the cuisine department have led your child to decide that nothing but spaghetti will do, Professor Worobey suggests going with the flow. Give your toddler the food she is insisting on—with other familiar, nutritious foods served alongside. Left to their own devices, toddlers almost always tire of their self-imposed single food diets on their own. But if you make that pizza crust into a forbidden fruit, you may be dealing with the same craving for much longer.

NOW THAT YOU KNOW

Bribe not. The best way to increase the stock of your toddler's beloved favorite food is to use it as a reward for eating something else. "Using foods as bribes gives them a lot of cache," explains Jennifer Fisher, Ph.D., assistant professor of pediatrics and nutrition at Baylor College of Medicine. Simply put the desired food on a plate with whatever else you're hoping your toddler will eat. Odds are, the favored food will be eaten first, but as long as the portion is small, your toddler will still be hungry and may be willing to branch out when that one item is gone.

If at first you don't succeed. Lots of research has been done on what it takes to introduce new foods to toddlers. It seems a combination of patience and persistence works best, explains Dr. Fisher. "Parents providing an example is very important, because children learn a lot about how and what to eat by watching their parents. If they see you enjoying a food, they're more likely to give it a try themselves."

In laboratory studies, toddlers can be quite open to trying new foods—they just need a long lead time to get used to them. Most toddlers offered the same foods eight to ten times—and not forced to eat them or bribed with treats—eventually come to like those foods all on their own. Not every child is going to come around to liking broccoli or zucchini or meatloaf, but many will if given the opportunity to discover them gradually.

A world of options. There's more than one way to get your toddler to eat his vegetables—in fact, there are thousands, says Harriet Worobey. "Don't let your toddler's refusal to eat cucumbers bother you—lots of people don't like cucumbers," she says. "The worst thing to do in this situation is to make a big deal about it. Instead, take a hard look at what your toddler *is* willing to eat and see if you can come up with something similar." A toddler who eats cantaloupe, for example, may be willing to eat sweet potato or mango or watermelon. Your child may only branch out in very small ways for a long time, so start with foods that are one step removed from those that have earned your tiny tyrant's stamp of approval, and work your way from there.

What they don't know. There are lots of ways for enterprising parents to slip nutritious foods into toddlers' diets in disguise. If your toddler is only willing to eat a couple things, give some thought to how you might enrich those foods with whatever food groups are being overlooked in his diet by mixing them with what he likes. Wheat germ in macaroni and cheese, zucchini in muffins, and grated carrot in spaghetti sauce are all tricks of moms desperate to make sure their toddlers eat a healthy diet, and the average child never even knows the intruding food was there. Each of my three children has delighted in eating green eggs and ham as a toddler—all blissfully unaware that that green stuff was spinach.

Invite a friend. If your toddler won't expand his diet for you, invite another child—one you know is a good eater—to come and share a few meals with him. Toddlers are natural mimics—most of all of their peers. If your child's buddies are willing to eat yogurt or cheese or bananas, he may decide to make the leap, too. In one study, a toddler who would eat corn but not peas was seated next to a child who would eat peas but not corn at several meals over the course of a week. By the end of the week, both children were happy to eat both peas and corn. Incidentally, parents are often amazed to discover that their toddlers eat foods at day care that they won't touch at home. If this is the case for your toddler, consider offering new foods in a social setting instead of at your kitchen table.

Chapter 17

WHY DO TODDLERS SWALLOW WITHOUT CHEWING?

I never thought there was anything scary about macaroni and cheese until my first-born child opened his throat and ate fistfuls of it as fast as he could, never so much as twitching his jaws in an attempt to chew. I stirred the macaroni in my own bowl; it seemed pretty gluey for such reckless consumption. Gazing again at my twenty-month-old, I could imagine the goo filling up his esophagus, spilling over to block his airways. I snatched the bowl from his tray.

Brendan looked at me for a few seconds, then slumped with his head on the tray in front of him, sobbing.

I had to decide then and there if I was going to be the kind of mom that takes away the noodles and lets her baby cry—or the kind that tries to undertake something so ridiculous and futile as trying to teach a young toddler to chew. A minute later, I was making exaggerated chewing motions, pointing to my own jaw, and Brendan had resumed eating in exactly the same manner as before.

There are several reasons toddlers swallow food without chewing, and one of them is that some days they eat as if they might starve. There are times when watching your toddler shovel down a meal is like watching a speed-eating competition. You just can't imagine scarfing food that way. For toddlers, though, eating jags are often tied to growth spurts.

The danger, of course, in eating like a maniac is that a child might choke. "The human body is provided with a number of defense mechanisms to keep airways free and clear," explains Michael Bye, M.D., professor of pediatrics and pulmonary medicine at Columbia University College of Physicians and Surgeons, "but none of those mechanisms is perfect, and small children are at much higher risk than the rest of us for aspirating a foreign object."

In addition to the pace at which they eat, there are several more reasons toddlers swallow without chewing, putting themselves in danger of choking. "Children's lack of molar teeth decreases their ability to chew sufficiently, leaving larger chunks of food," explains Dr. Bye. "Their propensity to talk, laugh, and run around while chewing also increases their risk."

What's more, children don't learn to fully control their jaws in the kind of thorough, side-to-side grinding motion adults use to chew their food until they are close to age four. They just don't have the muscle coordination in their mouths yet to do it.

Throw in proportionally small airways, and while the toddler years are already the most at-risk for choking, you'll begin to see that it's a small miracle every time your toddler successfully downs a meal. For the time being, his meals need come at times when you can sit, eat with him, and watch for any signs of difficulty. By the time he's four, his eating skills will begin to catch up with his appetite. Until then, you'll have to prepare his plate carefully and be ready to intervene if there's a problem.

💡 NOW THAT YOU KNOW

Try creative cutting. If your toddler is one who gulps down food without chewing, you need to take extra care to make sure everything that makes it to his plate is cut accordingly. Sometimes, a parent's first thought on how to cut a food is not the best bet. For example, Harriet Worobey, director of the Nutritional Sciences Preschool at Rutgers University, recommends cutting long foods into long, narrow strips—not into short, small circles or squares. "If you look at the pieces you end up with when you slice a hot dog crosswise, you'll see that they're about the size of marbles," she explains. "Cut hot dogs, carrots, and similar foods into narrow lengthwise strips, and let your toddler take bites from those pieces instead."

Sit still. Teach your toddler from the time she begins eating solid foods that meals take place only when she is sitting still at the table or in her high chair. Toddlers are like the friend who can't chew gum and walk at the same time. They need to give their full concentration to chewing and swallowing their food.

The usual suspects. According to Dr. Bye, the foods that most often get swallowed without sufficient chewing are pieces of meat and small, smooth items such as grapes, hot dogs, and sausages.

Unexpected culprits. Sometimes foods that seem small enough to pass through a toddler whole can still cause significant problems if they are not chewed. Things like dried fruits (especially raisins) and seeds often go down whole, but in the digestive tract, they absorb liquid until they can get large enough to create an obstruction. As silly as it may seem, cut raisins in half for your toddler and other dried fruits into small pieces. Size is not the issue you're dealing with, it's a food's capacity to absorb water and expand. Foods like sunflower seeds and most nuts are best left out of your toddler's diet altogether until age four or five.

Be prepared. Your best insurance against any serious problems resulting from a toddler's habit of swallowing food that hasn't been chewed enough is being prepared to perform the Heimlich maneuver or CPR if he does choke. Your second important resource is your own powers of observation. In one study, in as many as a third of cases where toddlers required medical attention for aspirating food or toys, the parents did not know that the object had been swallowed or swallowed whole. Possible warning signs that this may have happened to your toddler include wheezing, a persistent cough, and a sudden change in his voice.

Beware the high-risk eater. Some children struggle more with learning to chew properly than others. In many cases, because the muscles involved in manipulating the jaw and tongue are the same as those used in speech, these children may also lag a little behind their peers in language acquisition, too. If your child has a history of choking, gagging, or swallowing insufficiently chewed food, be sure all of his caregivers know about it and are prepared to cut his food into tiny pieces and pay enough attention while he's eating. If the problem is severe, ask your pediatrician about the possibility of being referred to a speech therapist who can help your toddler develop his oral skills.

Chapter 18

WHY DO TODDLERS SMEAR, STACK, JUGGLE, AND THROW THEIR FOOD?

To a toddler, a plate might as well be a blank canvas—one that extends to the tabletop, the chair, his own lap, and the floor. His paints are the foods you have lovingly prepared and arranged in shapes and color patterns in hopes that he'd find them attractive enough to eat.

You didn't really think this was all about eating, did you?

Food is about so much more than caloric satisfaction for children between one and three, it's hard to know where to begin. Rest assured, though, that the food on your carefully prepared plate is going to get poked, pushed, squeezed, smeared, and otherwise abused before, during, and after any consumption that might take place.

As messy and disappointing as it is, think of your toddler's time spent playing with his food as first lessons in physics, chemistry, and art. In fact, the tools on a small child's plate may very well offer up the most exciting toys he's got. What else is half as much fun to play and experiment with, and where else can a toddler get such great, dramatic reactions from Mom and Dad?

Your toddler undoubtedly has lots of toys that are visually stimulating, and probably many that are exciting to listen to, as well. But a toddler has five senses, and there is no better place to have fun with taste, smell, and touch than at the table.

"As adults, we enjoy smell, taste, and texture through our foods, too," says Harriet Worobey, director of the Nutritional Sciences Preschool at Rutgers University, "but we have learned socially acceptable ways to do that. We use utensils to help us taste, we smell our food without burying our noses in it, and we manage to appreciate texture in our mouths instead of with our hands. Toddlers are just beginning to learn social graces, and so they appreciate their foods in much more overt ways."

The question for parents usually boils down to, "How much of this are we supposed to take?"

The answer, most experts agree, is quite a lot. "For a child who is just entering the toddler stage, put a bib on him, spread plastic on the floor, and let him play," says Worobey. "If you are still spoon-feeding your two-year-old because you don't want him to make a mess, you are not doing either of you any favors. Give the child the spoon, give him a chance, and be prepared to clean up afterward. This is an important step for your toddler, and he has to find his way to it."

Fortunately, the period of time during which you need to let your toddler play with his food is limited. As they get closer to two and begin to show an interest in being more independent and in copying you, then it's time to start weaning them from playing with food.

According to Martha Farrell Erickson, Ph.D., Senior Fellow of the University of Minnesota's Children, Youth, and Family Consortium, this age is the ideal one to gradually limit food play to acceptable times, for example during preparation or with a limited list of foods. "You can help your toddler use cookie cutters to turn sandwiches or pancakes into animals before eating them, or let your toddler make his own hamburger patty," explains Dr. Erickson. "When they start playing with food in less appropriate ways, don't get angry, but offer an alternative, like 'Here, let's play with this Play-Doh and save your food for when you're hungry.'"

☼ NOW THAT YOU KNOW

Paint with pudding. Giving your toddler a chance to go all out in food play can be a liberating experience for you both—and a chance to start talking about times when he can and cannot get elbow-deep in his food. Finger-painting with pudding, making Fruit Loop necklaces, and sculpting edible dough all give kids a chance to play with food with your blessing, and that makes it all the more fun for them.

The banana stops here. Your expectations for the kind of table manners your toddler can manage should change as he gets older. For the under-two set, Harriet Worobey suggests starting with one simple rule: Don't throw food. "Throwing," Worobey explains, "is the thing that pushes a lot of parents over the edge—and not throwing is a concept that even a very young child can learn."

Don't take it away yet! Many parents subscribe to the mentality that if a child is playing with food, then the child is finished eating, and the meal is over. That isn't always the case. "Sometimes it does mean they are not going to eat their food," says Dr. Erickson, "but I've seen plenty of toddlers do things like mashing all their food together, or squishing a peanut butter sandwich into a little ball, before eating it."

Clean-up duty. After your toddler turns two, it's time to start giving him a fair share of clean-up duty after his meals. Actually, his fair share is probably cleaning it all himself, and that's not going to happen for years yet. By the age of two, your child can help and the opportunity to do so has a couple benefits over just lecturing him while you do it. First, he has an active role in taking care of the mess, and therefore a better appreciation of what he's done. Second, and more importantly, it teaches a toddler that cleaning up is what they should do when they make a mess. This is one of the basic lifetime skills you want your children to learn as early as possible, and with an eager-to-help toddler, it's easy to lay a foundation for taking care of his own messes that will carry over in adulthood.

Chapter 19

WHY DO TODDLERS TRY TO EAT PLASTIC GRAPES AND MUD PIES?

Of all the apples in the world, your toddler has to pick the wax display one in the furniture department at JCPenney. After running a quick mental tally of how many dirty hands have probably touched the darned thing in the years it's been on that coffee table—and wondering how well wax harbors bacteria—you take a close look at the fake fruit, which now has fresh tooth imprints. It doesn't feel or smell like a real apple. It's not the right weight. The only place where it's a fairly accurate representation is in the way it looks.

For your toddler, that's quite enough.

Tests have proven that children under the age of three don't make the kind of sophisticated distinctions between what things look like and what they actually are that older kids and adults do. In a study at Stanford University, toddlers were shown a sponge painted to look like a rock. Two- and three-year-olds almost unanimously concurred that the sponge was, indeed, a rock. Four- and five-year-olds could tell that something was up with that lightweight, funny-looking rock and share their doubts.

Dorothy Richmond, M.D., associate professor of pediatrics at Georgetown University, has seen this kind of misperception first-hand at home. "My two-year-old granddaughter came into the kitchen and found me juicing oranges," Dr. Richmond explains. "She was devastated. I couldn't make out all the words she was saying because she was very upset, but the upshot was that I was ruining the only thing these round, bright, orange things could be—toy balls."

Dr. Richmond's attempts at explaining what she was doing fell on deaf ears—because at two years old, what a child sees is all the explanation she can process. Eventually, the oranges were put away until after bedtime because Grandma didn't want to be thought of as a toy butcherer.

Without the ability to make quick distinctions between "is" and "looks like," toddlers learn by playing the averages when they encounter a new, but somehow familiar, object.

"The toddler did a quick mental calculation when he saw that apple, and decided that all the other apples he'd encountered so far tasted pretty good," explains DeDe Wohlfarth, Ph.D., assistant professor of psychology at Spalding University. "It turned out that this apple was a rare exception, but many toddlers, given another chance, will do the exact same thing again—after all, the yucky apple was not the norm."

It is only through experience that your toddler learns to distinguish things that are edible from stuff that just looks yummy. In the meantime, you'll have to guard her from the artificial fruit, and vice versa. Neither one is good for the other.

NOW THAT YOU KNOW

She makes a mean mud pie. By the time they turn three, most toddlers will look rather surprised, if not horrified, when they see a researcher take a bite of the Play-Doh they are pretending to make food from. (It's just one of the measures of devotion to science of investigators who study early childhood behavior that someone would bite Play-Doh for an experiment.) Before that age, however, many young toddlers look at Play-Doh, mud pies, clay—pretty much anything that they are pretending is food—as if it is food. They don't think twice about chomping down on the plastic fruit in their play kitchens, either. In the case of toddler-made food items, it's not so much their resemblance to real food that suckers them into tasting as their own imaginations. If your toddler tells you she's making any kind of food out of a nonfood item, it's time to make an assessment of how toxic it might be and to be ready to intervene before your toddler consumes it.

Plastic chicken and germs. In the interest of protecting your toddler from bacteria, their friends' germs, and the grime on their own hands, take the time to sterilize their toys that look like food (and eating utensils) from time to time. It only takes a minute to throw the tea set or the plastic food that came with that play kitchen in the dishwasher, but when it comes out you can watch your toddler relish her pseudo meal or tea party without worrying yourself sick about where it's been and what might be on it.

Pretty is as pretty tastes. Simulated foods are not the only attractive looking objects many toddlers are willing to try out for taste. Suzy Grant of Bedford, Texas, reported that a toddler she babysat for over a year in her home tried her best to eat the bubbles off the top of her bath. Other household substances that sometimes look good enough to eat to toddlers include soap, toothpaste, makeup, candles, and potted plants.

Just in case. The one important implication to keep in mind because your toddler doesn't know the difference between "looks like" and "is" is that some things that look edible and are not can pose choking and toxicity hazards. Keep close track of what goes into your toddler's mouth, and always have the numbers for the poison control center and your family's pediatrician by the phone in case you ever need them.

Chapter 20

WHY DO TODDLERS HAVE A LOVE/HATE RELATIONSHIP WITH THEIR UTENSILS?

Connor could eat a whole bowl of cereal with a spoon four months before he could walk. He was what his pediatrician called "food motivated." Despite his early promise in spoon feeding, Connor didn't master stabbing food with a fork until well after he was three. Much to the toddler's frustration, that second eating utensil was a whole lot harder to learn to use.

All toddlers learn to eat with utensils eventually, but some pick them up early, and others put them off as long as possible. Even the most determined and patient students, though, go through the love/hate thing with their silverware. They want to eat like Mom and Dad, but at some point they just want to eat, period. If their attempts at using a spoon or fork aren't getting the job done, some will drop them and fall back on their hands—others will demonstrate the kind of frustrated fury only a toddler can muster. Utensil-induced temper tantrums are for many kids just par for the course.

Child development experts and nutrition researchers are largely in agreement that there is no reason to push the eating utensil issue with any child under three. "By all means, you can offer your baby a spoon as soon as he is big enough to hold one," says Harriet Worobey, Director of the Nutrition Sciences Preschool at Rutgers University. "But let him figure out how to use it when he's ready."

Most toddlers start being able to effectively manipulate a spoon by the time they turn two, with success with a fork following as much as a year (or more) later. Ironically, it's sometimes the children whose parents are the most concerned with good manners who learn to use their utensils last, explains Professor Worobey. "If Mom is very worried about the toddler or the kitchen being a mess, she may not just hand her child a spoon and let him figure out what to do with it. Yes, things are going to get dirty and out of order while your toddler is learning how to eat with utensils, but yes, you have to go ahead and let him do it anyway."

While your toddler is grappling with utensils, your best bet is to offer help when he'll accept it, and to model proper table manners yourself the rest of the time. If your toddler sits down to at least one regular meal at the table with Mom, Dad or both every day of his life, and if Mom and Dad make a point to eat with the appropriate tools, say "please," "thank you," and "excuse me," and lead by example, he'll pick up those good manners almost by osmosis. When the eye-hand-mouth coordination skills required to use utensils finally come into alignment, toddlers who have been exposed to good table manners will have all the basic skills to have acceptable manners of their own.

NOW THAT YOU KNOW

Choosing the just-right utensils. Not just any utensils will do for a toddler trying to manage to eat on his own. Don't give him one of those baby spoons you used to feed him rice cereal. They are too small, may have plastic tips that make it harder to keep food on, and they don't hold enough of anything to make a decent bite for a toddler. Adult spoons are too large for toddlers' mouths, and the handles are too long for their hands. Choose a spoon with a wide surface area and a short, blunt handle for your toddler to start with—and have plenty of them on hand, as he may use more than one at a meal.

And the just-right plate. The main tool a toddler needs to go along with his spoon is a dish with a side he can push food against. Plates with flat edges are cruel when you're just learning how to scoop. Bowls are almost as hard.

Make a kid-friendly plate. Don't give your toddler a plate full of foods that all have to be eaten with a spoon or fork. It's just too much work for a beginner, explains Professor Worobey. "It's a good idea to offer a mix of finger foods and foods that require utensils in any given meal." Your aspiring fine-diner will try a little harder to use his utensils if they are for just one or two items on the plate, rather than a necessary evil for all of them. And if the food that needs a spoon is one of your toddler's favorites—like pudding or applesauce—he may try harder to make the utensils work for him.

Don't let things get out of hand. A utensil-related temper tantrum or two may be inevitable, but when you see your toddler's frustration level escalating, try to intervene before it reaches that point. Never try to take your toddler's utensil away to show him how to use it—they are his for the duration of the meal if he wants them. Instead, congratulate your toddler on the hard work he's done already, sympathize, and offer help using a set of your own utensils: "Boy, using a fork is hard work isn't it? You've done such a great job. Why don't you let your spoon take a break for just a minute and let Mommy help you?" You may get a vehement "NO" in response to your offer, but many toddlers, satisfied that you see their progress, are willing to accept assistance.

Don't laugh! As cute as your toddler's early attempts to eat with good manners may be (picking up a fistful of food and plopping it on the utensil is a very common survival technique), resist the temptation to laugh at your toddler's efforts. Some toddlers will be offended to find that you're giggling at something that's so hard for them. The majority, though, can change from hard-working student of good manners to class clown in a heartbeat. If something your toddler is doing makes you laugh, he may well decide to make it a part of his dinnertime repertoire for a long time to come. And as adorable as it was the first time your child licked his plate clean or tried to put his spoon in his nose, it's not something you'll be wanting to see again tomorrow—or worse yet, at Grandma's Sunday dinner.

Chapter 21

WHY DO TODDLERS EAT BEFORE THE BLESSING?

Toddlers eat before the blessing, and before their parents are ready to join them, because they're hungry. There's no mystery in the motivation. The better question is about why toddlers don't seem to have the ability to wait—not even long enough for a quick prayer—before satisfying that hunger.

In the frontal lobes of our brains, we all have a nerve center that controls what's called "inhibitory process"—in essence, our ability to control ourselves. A toddler's brain development doesn't get around to this area until the kinds of connections required for a child to do things like walk, eat, and begin to talk are already developed. Perhaps Mother Nature realizes there isn't much to inhibit until those skills are learned.

Once that part of the brain starts to noticeably develop somewhere around age two, however, it will benefit your toddler to practice his inhibitory skills. You can start by encouraging small, positive affirmations like learning not to interrupt, saying please before receiving desired objects, or giving thanks before eating a meal.

In one of the more inventive studies on preschool children in recent history, researchers at Stanford University in the 1960s used an experiment now widely known as The Marshmallow Test to assess the capacity of young children to inhibit their own behavior. During the test, a researcher brought each preschooler into a room and gave the child a marshmallow. The children were told they could eat the marshmallow right away if they wanted to. But if they waited while their host ran an errand they could have a second marshmallow when the researcher returned if they still had the first one.

The researcher was gone for fifteen minutes, and during that time, about two-thirds of the kids ate their marshmallows. Some of them gobbled them up immediately; some did their very best to wait, but couldn't; some went to great lengths to keep themselves from giving in, including putting the marshmallow behind their backs so they couldn't see it.

The one third of the children who waited did receive a second marshmallow, demonstrating that they were capable of delayed gratification.

Years later, as researchers followed the academic and personal trajectories of the marshmallow kids' lives, they were shocked at what they found. The preschool children who had held on to those first marshmallows scored an average of over *two hundred* points higher on their SATs than the ones who ate them. The children who waited experienced more personal success as well. It seemed that the ability to wait for (or in some cases, work for) what they want in little kids was a better predictor of success than any IQ test.

NOW THAT YOU KNOW

Hold the marshmallows. The marshmallow test wouldn't work on the vast majority of toddlers—fifteen minutes is an eternity to a two-year-old. Learning to defer gratification is something your toddler needs to work up to. If you start working with him now, though, he will be more polite and more patient as his skills gradually increase.

Keep it brief. Toddlers are just at the very beginning of learning to inhibit their own actions, and so it's not fair to expect them to wait long for their rewards. Keep your blessings brief and other required times of waiting to a minimum. By asking him to just wait a minute or two, you are helping your toddler practice deferring gratification. As he gets older, he'll be able to wait longer and work harder for the things he wants. For now, each small act of patience has its own reward: a meal after a prayer, your attention after waiting instead of interrupting, and so on.

The inimitable star chart. As your toddler gets bigger, you can gradually increase his concept of waiting for things he wants. Use a sticker chart your child can see to keep track of things he can (and does) do for himself—he might get stars for getting himself undressed before his bath, or for staying in his bed all night, for example. When he gets three stars (you can start to raise the number as his understanding of numerals gets better), give your toddler a treat like an extra story at bedtime, a time to play with clay, or a trip to the playground. If you follow through, your toddler will learn in a way he can see for himself how he benefits by cooperating and waiting for rewards.

Chapter 22

WHY DO TODDLERS
SPIT OUT FOOD?

Your mother most likely taught you not to spit. It's one of those items on the list of things a good mother must convey, right up there with "Keep your shoes off the furniture" and "Don't wipe your mouth on your sleeve."

Someday, you will teach your toddler not to spit, too. But not just yet.

For a little while longer, your toddler has good reasons to spit—reasons that take precedence over social acceptability. For the most part, toddlers spit so they don't gag or choke, though occasionally they will do it for more mischievous reasons.

"Spitting out food really is a necessary evil for toddlers," says Susan Nelson, M.D., assistant professor of family medicine at the University of Memphis Medical School. "Sometimes they do it reflexively; and at other times it is deliberate. But until they are a little older, it's something parents have to live with."

Part of the reason so much spitting goes on at this age is that toddlers get carried away with what and how much they put in their mouths. When something tastes good to them, they seem to use the old my-eyes-were-bigger-than-my-stomach logic adults use. But it's actually one better: "My eyes were bigger than my stomach, but I didn't figure that out until the food was already in my mouth." When it happens, they really have no choice but to spit.

Toddlers who bite off more than they can chew also make a bad habit of a behavior called "pouching." You've probably seen it already (and probably thought it was pretty gross) in your house. Toddlers put food in their mouths, tuck it into the corner, and hold it there indefinitely. It happens with foods they don't especially like, foods they like a lot, and with portions of foods they find hard to swallow like a particularly tough little piece of meat or a bit of peel from an apple.

One of the more difficult circumstances for parents to accept is the rejection of new foods, into which toddlers spit. Unfortunately, if you want your child to be willing to give new things a shot, you've got to be willing to let her spit them out if she doesn't approve, explains Dorothy Richmond, M.D., professor of pediatrics at Georgetown University Medical School. The spitting caveat is part of the deal: your toddler suspiciously puts this new, not-too-appealing looking item in her mouth, but you agree that she can immediately take it out if she finds it offensive.

When your toddler does spit out new foods, don't write them off just yet. It often takes several tries before a new food wins the approval of a finicky young eater. Your toddler's taste-and-spit experiment does count as one of those critical tries. Next time, the same food may go over much better.

NOW THAT YOU KNOW

Why ask why? Motive is everything when it comes to deciding whether or not to give your toddler a hard time about spitting. If the reason is any of those listed above, or if you have even an inkling that there was a gag or other unpleasant physical reflex coming, give your toddler the benefit of the doubt and don't say a word. If, however, your toddler takes a mouthful of Cheerios, apple juice, or anything else, then spits at you, the floor, the dog, or anyone else, you have found the place where you must draw the line.

Spitting at anyone, or spitting and then checking to see if it's working in getting a rise out of Mom, needs to receive a swift, calm, negative response. Immediately tell your toddler, "No, we do not spit like that," wipe his mouth, take away the food he's using for his arsenal, and give him as little attention as possible for the next two minutes. Chances are very good that once your toddler sees that that kind of spitting results in loss of both his meal and his dining companion, he'll give it up.

Spit etiquette. You have to accept spitting as part of life with a toddler, but you can influence how offensive it has to be. Even a young toddler can begin to learn how to spit discreetly if you teach him. If you keep a close eye on your toddler while he's eating, very soon you'll know when there's a spit coming. (I'm sure it's one of the tell-tale signs of parenthood that we have a hand-under-chin reflex when our kids are about to spit.) As soon as you see that your child is having trouble with a food, or that he just doesn't like it, put a napkin in front of his mouth and tell him to spit it in the napkin. Some parents give their toddlers a spit cup or bowl just for this purpose, but a napkin makes more sense if you're planning to eat in front of people anytime in the near future. After your toddler has successfully spit on command a few times, set his place with a napkin at each meal. When he needs to spit out food, show him how to grab his own napkin and use it. If your toddler slips up and spits in his lap or on the table, let him help you clean up with a napkin, but don't say anything negative about the mistake. If you're patient and consistent, your child will learn to spit food out without making a scene—and even though spitting out food drops off as we get older, that's still a "skill" he'll use for a lifetime.

Chapter 23

WHY DO TODDLERS FALL ASLEEP WHILE THEY'RE STILL EATING?

It's a sad, sad scene. One minute your toddler is greedily gobbling up spaghetti, and the next his eyelids suddenly get heavy and against all odds he puts his head down in the plate, snoring softly. There are noodles in his hair and in his ears, in addition to the usual collection on his hands, arms, chin, and lap. How could this happen?

Most of us don't see adults falling asleep in the middle of a meal. Well, maybe we see the chin-on-chest kind of sleep from your grandfather, but not the face-on-plate variety. It is fairly unique to toddlers, and all too common.

According to Dorothy Richmond, M.D., an associate professor of pediatrics at Georgetown University, toddlers fall asleep in their plates for the same reason they wear diapers and require constant supervision. Their little brains are not quite capable yet of anticipating what is coming next. If you think about it, a person who doesn't have the mental ability to know that he'd better hustle to the bathroom because his bladder is full can't really be expected to know he has to go lay down before he nods off. "Toddlers are powerless to prevent these things," says Dr. Richmond. "They can't tell the difference between needing to sleep and sleeping. Bodily functions just happen *to* them—whether they're ready or not."

Face-in-plate sleeping is a particularly common example of a toddler's inability to predict for another reason. When he was an infant, there was no more sure bet than a full belly to help him nod off. He's a busy "big kid" now, but the comfort factor of satisfied hunger can still have a powerful sedative effect.

"What often happens at this age is that toddlers race from one thing to the next, even when they're very tired—especially when they're tired," explains Dr. Richmond. "They get so caught up in being busy that sometimes they can't seem to sleep, even when they need it." Stopping to eat and feeling full can be the one thing that intervenes in that cycle of go, go, go, and once it's broken, some toddlers almost immediately drop off to sleep, with no consideration for whether their head will rest on a feather pillow or one made of peanut butter and jelly sandwich.

Now That You Know

Lunchtime is lunchtime is lunchtime. The easiest way to avoid having your wiped-out toddler crash out at a meal is to make sure he's on a predictable eating and sleeping schedule. Toddlers are very much creatures of habit, and if they have breakfast, lunch, dinner, and snacks every day at around the same time—as well as naps and bedtime at regular times—they will be less likely to nod off mid-meal.

The schedule thing works the other way around as well. A toddler who falls asleep one day during lunch may conk out at the very same time (and in the very same place) for several days after. If this mix-up happens at your house, temporarily move the meal in question up a half hour to try to get your child back to an eat first, sleep after routine. Once you've had three days of meal, then sleep, you can start inching the mealtime back to the time you prefer by ten minutes a day.

Handle with care. Some toddlers gorge themselves just before conking out—as if their body knows there's only a limited amount of time to ingest as much as possible—and it's not uncommon for them to have a mouth full of food at the moment they fall asleep. This can put your child in danger of choking. If your toddler nods off while eating, do a finger-sweep of the inside of his mouth to make sure there is no food in there that could pose a hazard.

Now what? What to do with a food-spattered, upright, sleeping toddler is always a dilemma. No parent in their right mind wants to wake up a child who's *that* tired, but you can't very well leave them the way they are, either. In the afternoon, if your toddler eats in a high chair and is securely strapped in, you can make him as comfortable as possible after you make sure his mouth is empty. In any kind of chair a toddler can slide out of, though, he's going to have to be moved. One mom keeps a beach towel handy to throw on the couch for just this purpose; another uses a nap mat on the floor. The less distance you have to take your toddler—and the less scrubbing you decide to do before you put him there—the more likely he'll get a decent nap out of it.

At night, you have to weigh the benefits of letting your toddler nap at the expense of your own sleep later. A fair compromise is to let your toddler sleep ten or fifteen minutes at the table, a power nap to get him through to bedtime (which will also give you the opportunity for some clean-up), then wake him up for the remainder of the evening.

part three

So Little Sleep

Chapter 24

WHY DO TODDLERS WAKE UP
SO DARNED EARLY?

Did you know that a rat, with an average life expectancy of two to three years, will be dead within three weeks if completely deprived of sleep? All the ridiculously busy parents are looking at their watches, looking at the calendar, and wondering just how fast their own clocks are ticking. For many of us, sleep deprivation is a way of life. We know all about the early to bed, early to rise routine, but finding a night when we can actually go to bed early is a challenge most of us never meet.

Now, getting *up* early is another story. We all do that. We do it because our precious children, the ones who actually have a God-given entitlement to take naps, make sure we get up and at 'em every day at the crack of dawn.

Toddlers who get up first thing in the morning can usually be divided into two camps: those who are happy about it, and those who can't help themselves.

Toddlers who wake up cheerful, rested, and ready to start the day do so because they have (no surprise here) already had enough sleep. For some toddlers, this moment comes after twelve hours of snoozing; for others, it comes after ten or even less. If your toddler is one of these, you should be congratulated on having a healthy, happy child on her appropriate sleep schedule. The bad news is, her sleep schedule doesn't quite jibe with yours.

The second group is toddlers who wake up still tired. They wake up grumpy, groggy, and within an hour or two, they may be right back in bed, sprawled on the couch watching TV, or on the verge of a temper tantrum. According to Jodi Mindell, Ph.D., associate professor of psychology at St. Joseph's University in Philadelphia and author of *Sleeping Through the Night*, toddlers who wake up too early and act this way may need to have their bedtime moved up an hour, or even more, earlier. It goes against parental logic to put a kid to bed earlier in hopes that she'll sleep later, but in the case of kids who are chronically overtired, that's exactly what needs to happen.

"Sometimes parents are amazed at how much more pleasant their kids are once they're getting enough sleep," says Dr. Mindell. Small wonder that grown ups with children didn't already know *that*.

NOW THAT YOU KNOW

Reset your toddler's clock. You can't make a healthy, happy toddler sleep more, but you can try to adjust his schedule to work better with yours. For starters, time your child's nap for a few days to see how much (if any) of his daily sleep requirement is being met during daylight. If that time is anything over an hour, consider cutting it back. Next, look at bedtime. If you have a toddler who doesn't require a long night's sleep, you may have to decide whether you'd rather have your little bit of peace and quiet at night or your extra bit of sleep in the morning.

To push back a toddler's bedtime, you'll need to keep a close eye on the clock. Start the entire bedtime routine fifteen minutes later than usual, winding up with lights-out at fifteen minutes past normal. A week after the first fifteen-minute move, you can add another fifteen minutes. Ideally, your toddler will sleep a little later for each missing increment of sleep. The method is not foolproof, but for many children it works.

Let's play—go ahead and start without me. A second option for stealing a bit more sleep from an early-rising toddler is giving him a game or job to do when he first wakes up. Try providing a "morning bag" for your toddler to play with each day when he wakes. Sometime during each day, put a few books and toys into a bag or box labeled with your child's name and "Morning Games." (Be sure to use a container that will not pose a choking or suffocation threat to your child: no plastic, no drawstrings.) Don't let your toddler help you or watch you fill the bag, and don't show it to him. After your child goes to bed, put the morning bag next to his crib or bed. For the first couple days, you'll have to show your toddler how to go to the bag upon waking and play with its contents. After a few days of pleasant surprises, though, he may well decide to tackle the morning bag and play on his own.

Darkness helps. If your toddler wakes every morning when the first rays of light stream through his window, it's hard to argue with his basic circadian logic. Sometimes simply installing heavy shades or drapes can help toddlers sleep a little later—especially children who seem to be waking up when they are still tired.

Bridging the gap. To help a toddler who isn't sleeping late enough to doze a little longer each morning, try beating him to the punch for a few days. Half an hour before your little one normally wakes up, tiptoe into his room with your pillow and lay down beside his crib or bed. When he opens one eye and sees that you're already there (no need to get up and call or make his way to your room), some toddlers will just sigh and go back to sleep. Once they have managed to keep sleeping until a later hour a couple days in a row, many children will stick to the new schedule—even without your presence next to the bed.

Chapter 25

WHY DO TODDLERS STOP TAKING NAPS WHEN THEY STILL NEED THEM?

On Tuesday afternoon, twenty-two-month-old Junior breaks with tradition: he plays in his crib instead of taking a nap. On Thursday, he goes one better and climbs out (a somewhat unfortunate new skill) and comes to visit you during naptime. His demeanor as he rounds the corner into the kitchen is all bravado—a look-ma-no-crib grin from ear to ear.

Have you just lost the last significant bastion of peace and quiet in your daylight hours?

Parenting experts almost unanimously agree that no, you have not. "Most children under three still need naps," says Edward Christophersen, Ph.D., clinical psychologist and professor of pediatrics at the University of Missouri at Kansas City School of Medicine and author of *Parenting That Works: Building Skills that Last a Lifetime*. The vast majority of toddlers need an afternoon rest time, he explains, even if they do not sleep.

More than 80 percent of toddlers do need and get sleep at naptime; in fact, those eighteen months and younger often still need two naps each day. Toddlers ranging from just-walking to almost-three are learning and growing at such breakneck speed that they require the extra sleep to rejuvenate, even on what seems like an uneventful day.

If your toddler decides to play in bed instead of sleeping one day, there's no reason to make a big deal of it, Dr. Christophersen explains. "He may be tired later, or he may just not need a nap that day, but if he has stayed in the right place and amused himself, then he hasn't done a single thing wrong. No matter how hard you try, you can't really make another person sleep."

If your toddler is wandering the house, though, it's time to lay down one or two simple naptime rules. The big one, of course, is that naptime takes place, from beginning to end, in your toddler's bed (or his room, if you want to allow him a little more space). Tell your child he must stay there for a specific amount of time—an hour is plenty for a toddler who is spending part of naptime playing, but some children need closer to two hours. Set a timer or alarm to go off so your toddler will be able to hear it at the end of naptime. That way there will be no confusion about when the nap is over. If Junior starts making a habit of playing at this time, allow him to bring a few safe toys or picture books to bed with him.

If your toddler makes a break for it, immediately take him back to bed, with as little conversation as possible. Tell him, "You have to stay in your room during naptime," and leave it at that. If necessary, you can use a baby gate (you'll need a tall one, or two stacked, if your toddler is adept at climbing out of a crib) to keep him safely in his room.

Even if your toddler doesn't seem to need a nap for the extra sleep, he needs one so you or your child-care provider can have a chance to recharge and refresh for the next round. Taking care of a toddler is a demanding job, and getting a chance to have a few adult moments in the afternoon can be the difference between a parent who is able to stay calm, even, and enthusiastic through the end of the day and one who is tired and temperamental.

NOW THAT YOU KNOW

Mind the clock. The key to keeping the nap in naptime is making sure it comes at the very same time and follows the same routine each day—

whether your toddler sleeps or not. As long as you don't give your toddler the impression that this period of time is negotiable, it will be easier to keep it as part of his regular routine.

Playing the averages. Every child's sleep requirements are different, so your toddler's behavior should be your first guide to how much sleep she needs. As a general rule, though, toddlers at eighteen months of age need about thirteen hours a day—ideally eleven at night, and two during a nap. By age three, that requirement for most children has dropped by an hour, with many children either sleeping less at night or taking a shorter nap.

Catching up. Some toddlers who assert they don't need a nap change their minds much later—late afternoon or dinnertime. If your toddler falls asleep far outside your scheduled naptime, give him thirty minutes, then wake him up. A very late nap can ruin the bedtime routine, but immediately waking up a wiped-out toddler won't do you any good either. Letting him have half a nap is a compromise that can work for both of you.

Chapter 26

WHY DO TODDLERS GET HYPER WHEN THEY'RE TIRED?

Talk about your reverse psychology. When you or I feel tired, we wind down until we conk out (or have another cup of coffee). A tired body, it seems, does eventually run out of steam.

Not so with many toddlers. For small children, exhaustion is like fuel, winding them tighter and tighter, until their actions are physically frantic, emotionally pitched, and ever on the brink of either a hysterical giggle fit or a big fat temper tantrum.

"With toddlers and preschoolers, the result of being sleep-deprived is getting all wound up—like the feeling adults have when we get a second wind," says Jodi Mindell, Ph.D., associate professor of psychology at St. Joseph's University in Philadelphia and author of *Sleeping Through the Night*. "Contrary to what it seems your child is trying to tell you, this means that if your toddler is acting wild late in the day, you may need to move up his bedtime."

Moving up bedtime for a toddler isn't nearly as hard as it sounds. "Kids this age are not attending to the clock," says Dr. Mindell. "That's the glory of toddlerhood." If your toddler starts getting out of control in the evenings as his exhaustion level ticks up, start his usual bedtime routine earlier. For some children, you can make a jump of a full half-hour or more without much resistance. For others, creeping the bedtime up in ten-minute increments seems to work better.

"Parents are often astounded at how much easier life is with a toddler once the child is getting enough sleep," says Dr. Mindell.

Getting your toddler from wired to tired can take some effort, but as you ease her into a routine where she is getting enough sleep, that can often make the difference between wild or willing at bedtime.

For starters, Dr. Mindell recommends instituting a regular, predictable bedtime ritual that includes things your toddler can enjoy and look forward to. "The whole thing should take between twenty and thirty minutes, and include three or four activities, in order, that appeal to your toddler," she explains. "Make sure that your routine also addresses every conceivable issue that might hold up bedtime when you get to the bed: a drink or snack if you allow them at bedtime, a chance to go potty if you're potty training, having an opportunity to say good-night to every member of your household." If you incorporate it all in your bedtime ritual, you'll have less stalling when the big, lights-out moment arrives.

Most of all, if your routine slips for one night or a few and you find your toddler acting out and getting wild at the end of the day again, don't punish her for being exhausted, and don't treat bedtime as if it's a punishment. If everyone in your family treats time to get ready for bed as a matter-of-fact part of the routine—one that they look forward to—then your toddler will learn to treat it that way, too.

"I'm always amazed when I go to the mall or the movies or out to dinner on a Friday night and see these toddlers who are throwing tantrums and running around going nuts and crying their hearts out," Dr. Mindell says. "The thing that's wrong with their behavior is not that they are being naughty, it's that they should already be in bed."

NOW THAT YOU KNOW

A time for running around, a time for settling down. Toddlers who don't get enough physical exercise and excitement during the day can be particularly over-stimulated at bedtime, almost as if their bodies take a use-it-or-lose-it approach to their daily energy allotment. Be sure your toddler has plenty of opportunity to run, jump, climb, and expend his energy during the day. For the last hour before bedtime, though, start trading off the energetic activities for quiet ones: building with blocks, reading books, scribbling on paper, things that will cue your toddler's busy body that things are winding down for the day.

Move in the right direction. Dr. Mindell suggests plotting your bedtime routine in terms of geography as well as intent. "You should always be moving in the right direction—toward your toddler's bed," she says. In other words, once you've gone to the section of the house where the bedrooms are, no part of your routine should take you back out of it; once you're in your toddler's room, you're there for the duration; and once your child has been coaxed into her bed, there should be no reason for her to get out.

Pretend to go to sleep. Some parents have great success at bedtime with games that get their toddlers to "pretend" bedtime. If your toddler has a vivid imagination, she may relish the opportunity to "play sleep" as part of her routine. Arrange your toddler's bedding in a circle for a "nest" and put your "baby bird" in it for the night; ask your toddler what animal they feel like today, and then tell her how that animal sleeps and let her mimic it; tell her that princesses sleep in pretty pink pajamas just like hers, and help her get costumed for bed.

Bedtime is not one size fits all. It is true that for many toddlers, stories at bedtime are a great settling-down tool, but it is equally true that some toddlers do not have any interest in being read to before bed. "The components of your routine don't matter nearly as much as the fact that they work for your individual child," says Dr. Mindell. For a very active child, for example, a component of bedtime might be putting his toys to bed for the night, making the rounds to make sure all the lights are off, or helping to get the dog settled in its bed. For one who loves to snuggle, turn off all the lights and tell a made-up bedtime story while your toddler mans a flashlight. For one who is very musical, climb into bed together and listen to a few favorite, quiet, songs, or sing a bedtime song together.

When the bedtime routine is done, it's time for you to leave and for your toddler to fall asleep alone. It may take some time to work up to this point, but if you keep the same enjoyable, predictable routine each night, it won't take your child long to learn that it's possible to sleep by himself after all.

Chapter 27

WHY DO TODDLERS BANG THEIR HEADS?

There are few among us who can't appreciate the pleasures of a good rocking chair, especially after a year or two of rocking babies. Many a nursing mom has fallen sound asleep lulled by the back-and-forth rhythm of a rocker, and many toddlers still jump at the chance to snuggle in Mom's lap in that same chair.

As strange as it seems, toddlers who deliberately bang their heads, especially at bedtime, seem to be trying to achieve the same kind of result. In the eyes of child development researchers, head banging, rocking back and forth, and head rubbing are all the same kind of behavior—self-comforting measures that, though no one understands exactly why they offer comfort, all stimulate the vestibular system that controls a body's balance from the inner ear.

As much as we can all relate to a rocking chair's charms, it's hard to imagine how head banging, often a very rapid, loud process during which the toddler bangs his head as many as sixty times a minute, could be comforting. However, since most of the children who do it use the habit to help themselves fall asleep, it seems to calm them all the same.

According to the American Academy of Pediatrics, head banging and rocking are actually quite common, with between 5 and 15 percent of children doing one or the other—or both—before age two. In many of those kids, the habit starts during infancy, often as early as six months of age.

As alarming as it is for parents to see their toddlers do something that seems potentially harmful, toddlers rarely, if ever, injure themselves any more seriously than creating a bruise by banging their heads. Even though it looks like what your toddler is doing must hurt, this is what pediatricians call a "self-limiting" behavior—your child will stop on his own before he hurts himself.

The majority of toddlers who bang their heads do not have any developmental problems. If your little rocker is otherwise healthy and well-adjusted, chances are he'll outgrow it soon.

A small percentage of toddlers who bang their heads do have developmental delays, and an even smaller number are autistic. Because of the small probability of another, more serious problem related to head-banging, explains Angela Camasto, M.D., a pediatrician in private practice in Easton, Pennsylvania, you should mention the habit to your toddler's pediatrician so he or she can make a full assessment.

NOW THAT YOU KNOW

Boys will be boys. More than two thirds of children who bang their heads are boys. No one knows for sure why boys lean toward this behavior more often than girls, but if your little linebacker is particularly zealous about it, his pediatrician may suggest he wear a helmet at times when he likes to bang his head.

Bang, bang, bang in other ways. There is something about a good, strong beat that appeals to your toddler, or he wouldn't have taken up this unusual way of putting himself at ease. Helping him find other ways to explore rhythms may help him replace his banging behavior in the long run (at least until he gets old enough to start wandering through life wearing a fully-amped CD player). Invest in a small set of hand-played drums, or try playing different kinds of music for your toddler to see what he likes. Although it has never been proven effective in a research setting, some parents even report that putting a metronome in their toddler's room can help take some of the intensity out of head banging.

Invest in a child-sized rocking chair. Another way to help your child discover alternative ways to comfort himself is to offer other opportunities not just to hear, but to feel rhythm. Putting a child-sized rocker in your child's room will give him an alternative way to stimulate his vestibular system that doesn't involve bonking his head. Don't try to force a child to switch from one of these behaviors to the other, but show him that rocking at tired times feels good, too.

Focus on other things. As disconcerting as head banging is, if you spend a lot of time talking about it with your toddler, talking about it with other people in front of your toddler, or trying to prevent it, your child will quickly learn that it's a fine method for getting your attention. Try to stay as low key as you can about your child's habit. To make it easier on yourself, you can rearrange his room by pulling the bed away from the wall, putting a mattress on the floor (so there is no headboard), or thoroughly padding the inside of the crib. Don't explain your reasons for doing these things to your toddler, but do let him help you redecorate, so he won't be put off by the changes.

A sign of other things? If your toddler has just begun head banging, or if his head-banging habit has become more intense in recent days, make an appointment to have his ears checked by the pediatrician. Although many children routinely bang their heads with no medical reason, some studies have linked the habit to discomfort from ear infections and from teething. In a move similar to an adult who bangs his fist to cope with an injury to another part of the body, some toddlers seem to be trying to take the edge off the pain of another ailment by banging their heads.

Chapter 28

WHY WON'T TODDLERS SLEEP ALONE?

We all come into this parenting thing knowing we're going to lose some sleep. Infants need to eat at all hours, and there's not a thing an exhausted parent can do but keep getting up and feeding them.

But when your baby becomes a toddler, a person who can ambulate on two feet, who can laugh at a funny face, and who occasionally eats enough in a sitting to hold her over for a couple days, then it doesn't seem fair anymore if Mom and Dad are still not getting a decent night's sleep. If your toddler can't fall asleep or stay asleep without you, chances are it becomes a bigger issue with every passing month.

"When your toddler can't fall asleep without you, it's usually just a matter of habit," says Jodi Mindell, Ph.D., associate professor of psychology at St. Joseph's University and author of *Sleeping Through the Night.* "Without intending to, you have made yourself your toddler's transition object—like a special blanky or a pacifier, you've become the 'thing' she needs to get to sleep."

There are almost as many schools of thought on the way to handle a toddler who won't sleep alone as there are pediatricians, but many parents find the two big, opposing theories just do not work for them at home. On the one hand, there are those who tell us to go ahead and let our toddlers sleep in our beds at their leisure, that we should be able to sleep just fine while they are visiting, that it's a happy, healthy arrangement for everyone. For some families it is. For others, every night the toddler shares the parents' bed means starting yet another morning dead tired.

At the opposite end of the spectrum are advisors who tell you to cut that kid's nighttime attention off right now, before the situation gets any worse. Put your toddler in her bed, they say, walk away, and don't look back. Plug your ears, mind you, because if your toddler has been keeping you up at night with cosleeping, crying for you at all hours, or making late-night visits to your bed, she is not going to take this arrangement lying down. She's going to scream, and you're going to feel like you have reached rock bottom as a parent—at least for the few nights it takes for your toddler to get over this cold-turkey approach to nighttime comfort from her parents.

Dr. Mindell suggests a middle-of-the-road approach, one that helps toddlers get to sleep and stay asleep alone, but doesn't force parents to turn a deaf ear to their distress. "For parents who don't want to use the quick and dirty method of letting their children cry themselves to sleep for as long as it takes, you can accomplish the same thing gradually," she explains. "Put your toddler to bed, but don't lay down beside her. If your toddler is used to having you hold her or stay with her in her bed until she falls asleep, start by sitting on the edge of the bed. Once she is comfortable with that change, move a few feet away, but stay where she can see you." You will receive protest for moving away, but in most cases, if you stay calm, quiet, and boring as a companion, your toddler will still drop off to sleep. After a few days, move a little closer to the door, still where your toddler can see you and know you are there.

The keys to success are staying consistent and trying to work within your toddler's threshold for change. Some children will be comfortable with a parent moving a little farther away every night; others will need a few nights to get used to each change. Although this kind of transition takes time, if you hold the ground you gain with each successive move, you and your toddler will soon both be sleeping comfortably—and separately—through the night.

NOW THAT YOU KNOW

Start at the beginning. The problem of a toddler who can't sleep through the night without you needs to be addressed first at bedtime, says Dr. Mindell. "Sometimes parents try to tackle this issue in the middle of the night—because that's when it really gets to be a problem that your toddler needs you to fall asleep." The best solution is to back up and look at the bigger picture instead, though. "If you teach toddlers to fall asleep at bedtime without you," Dr. Mindell explains, "they typically start to be able to get through the night without you, too."

Give her a new bed buddy. If your toddler is in the habit of snuggling with you at bedtime, try giving her a new transitional object for bedtime. It could be a stuffed toy or doll, a special blanket, or even an item of your clothing. Whether the object is your favorite sweatshirt or a Pooh, sleep with it next to you in your bed one night before presenting it to your toddler. Toddlers often take a great deal of comfort in familiar smells, and having yours in bed with them will help you ease out of the sleep routine.

Don't give up ground. No matter how much progress you make with your toddler, there will be a night soon when she has a bad dream or a fever, and you'll want or need to change the rules. If you bring her to your bed, you may have to start back at square one, and should do so as soon as the extenuating circumstances are over. Dr. Mindell recommends that parents use their own bed as a last resort, though. "Instead of moving your toddler to you, go to her," she suggests. If you go and sleep on the floor in your toddler's room, or even in her bed, her road back to sleeping by herself will be faster and easier on both of you than if you completely disrupt her routine by taking her out of her regular sleeping space.

Chapter 29

WHY DO TODDLERS *STILL*
WAKE UP AT NIGHT?

Oh the things the baby monitor can see. Emily's parents were on the verge of a major tiff about why the little girl's room wasn't picked up before bed at night when her mom realized the only possible culprit was the twenty-month-old toddler herself. Because Emily had never demonstrated the ability to climb out of her crib before, it just took a while for her parents to realize she must have figured it out. The couple picked up a video monitor at Wal-Mart and set it up in their daughter's room. Late that night, after taking turns keeping an eye on the monitor since their own bedtime, the incredulous couple watched on the monitor as their daughter's rather unusual "sleep" routine unfolded. After waking up around 1:30 in the morning and lying in her crib for a while, Emily carefully climbed out, stepping over to a well-placed doll house to ease her way to the floor. She teetered on her toy box to turn on the light, and proceeded to play quietly with just about every toy she owned. An hour later, she cautiously stepped back up onto the roof of the doll house and flopped back down in her crib. In a few minutes she was asleep, again, with the light still on.

Most parents can't imagine the luxury of a child who not only entertains herself when she wakes at night, but also falls back to sleep on her own. Kids like Emily are one in a million.

Truth be told, we all wake up at night. Some of us get up and go to the bathroom; some hike up the blankets, roll over, and fall back asleep. One study of young children found that they became fully awake an average of two times each night. Ask any harried mom of a toddler who doesn't know how to get himself back to sleep in the night, and you'll find out that some children wake up much more frequently than just twice.

It's not the toddler waking up that's a problem, per se, explains Edward Christophersen, Ph.D., clinical psychologist and professor of pediatrics at the University of Missouri at Kansas City School of Medicine. "It's what they do while they're awake." If your toddler doesn't think he can be awake—and go back to sleep—without you, *then* you have a problem.

Getting your toddler to stay in his own bed after waking at night is tricky business, but it has to start with a solid, predictable bedtime routine (for more on how, see Chapters 26 and 28). Once that's done, you need to decide how you're going to handle middle-of-the-night wakings and carve those rules in stone. Once your toddler is clear on what you will or will not allow when he wakes at night, both of you can move on with the business of getting your beauty rest.

☀ NOW THAT YOU KNOW

Cry baby. If you have established a bedtime routine that has your toddler falling asleep without you holding him, sleeping beside him, or otherwise serving as his favorite snuggly toy, then you may be surprised at just how brief his nighttime crying jags will be if you don't rush to the rescue when he wakes. Many parents, not prepared for the full-fledged tantrum-level crying they've seen in their toddlers at bedtimes past, jump in before the crying really kicks in. If your toddler has come far enough to fall asleep without you at bedtime, though, chances are very good he'll quickly do the same in the middle of the night if you give him just a little time to get over his initial cry.

If you must go . . . If the crying persists, or if you can't stand the thought of it, grab your pillow, go to your toddler's room, lie down where he can see you, and either really go to sleep or do your best imitation. Your presence will provide the security your toddler is craving, but by staying silent and setting the example of sleeping, you'll leave little for him to do but follow suit. If he's a sociable little guy, he may try to initiate conversation, but if you give in you risk helping your child confuse this part of nighttime with a social hour. If your toddler seems a little panicked because you're not talking, tell him once, calmly and quietly, that he is fine, you are tired, and this is a time for sleeping. The less fun and excitement you bring on your nighttime trip to your toddler's bedside, the less reason he'll have to invite you back tomorrow.

See what you can do in daylight. All behavior problems seem less daunting and dramatic in daylight, even sleep problems. If your toddler can't seem to help herself get settled back to sleep at night, take a close look at what she is or is not doing for herself during the day, suggests Dr. Christophersen. "Children who learn to amuse themselves and overcome small frustrations during the day often are very good at doing the same thing at night," he explains. "The advantage to working on this during the day is that both parent and child are more relaxed and open to trying a new tactic. At night, everyone's nerves are frayed."

To try this at home, ensure that your toddler spends some time playing alone each day. It's easy to fall into the role of permanent playmate—especially if this toddler is an only child—but being at the beck and call of a little guy during the day or every minute from the time you get home from work sets up the expectation that you'll take on that role the rest of the time, too. If your toddler gets frustrated with a game or toy, give him some time to try to calm himself before you come to the rescue. The sense of self-reliance you help him find will make playtime, and bedtime, easier on both of you.

If your toddler comes to you. Vagabond toddlers, wandering the house in search of companionship, comfort, and sometimes snacks in the middle of the night, are more than an impediment to your good night's sleep, they're a danger to themselves. If your child prowls the house at night— or even comes unwelcome to haunt your bedside—consider putting a gate across his doorway. Some parents despise the idea of a gate, but if you're open to the possibility, it makes it possible for your toddler to be safely contained without having to suffer the isolation of a closed door. Without the run of the house, many toddlers decide there's not much to do in the middle of the night but sleep, after all.

Chapter 30

WHY DO TODDLERS WIGGLE ENDLESSLY IN THEIR SLEEP?

Some toddlers close their eyes at bedtime and don't move a muscle until morning, doing their best lump imitation for the entire night. For others, though, the sleeping hours are almost as active as the waking ones have been. Your toddler may roll, sprawl, kick, reach, flip, and generally give herself a good workout, even while she's out like a light. Parents who have toddlers who wiggle, wriggle, and squirm the night away are often the first to find a way to help their children sleep all night in their own beds—it's a self-preservation measure for anyone who has ever slept at the mercy of a restless toddler who has commandeered a queen-sized bed.

The biggest reason toddlers tend to wiggle endlessly in their sleep is because they are so physically busy during the day that their bodies have a hard time completely shutting down—even when they're supposed to be at rest, explains Angela Camasto, M.D., a pediatrician in private practice in Easton, Pennsylvania. Your toddler's brain is busy processing all she's learned during the day while she gets her requisite sleep, and part of that process sometimes includes re-creating the movement challenges she's been grappling with.

When you hear your toddler rustling around in bed, or even crying for a few minutes in the night, don't sprint to her side to help her fall asleep again. There's a good chance she will manage to do that all on her own. Every time your toddler settles herself back to sleep after waking in the night brings her one step closer to the sigh-and-roll-over wake-ups most adults have throughout the night.

Unless your toddler is being kept awake by her own activity at night, all you need to do is ensure her safety and comfort needs have been addressed. Make sure she's wearing pajamas that will keep her warm after she's kicked off all her blankets (footie pajamas are the best solution in winter), and double check that there's nothing a busy girl could get tangled in overnight in the bed or crib. Once those goals are accomplished, don't let your toddler's restless sleep pattern interfere with your own snooze. Unless your toddler consistently wakes up seeming as if she is not rested, there's a very good chance that the only family member bothered by her restless sleep is you.

💡 NOW THAT YOU KNOW

Choose the best bed. Some parents hold off on moving their toddler to a big bed because of restless sleep patterns. This is a reasonable option as long as your toddler is not at risk of hurting herself while climbing out of the crib. If your child does climb out, you still don't have to hustle her out of the crib if you're not ready. Instead, invest in a "crib tent" that straps onto the sides of the crib and domes over the top. Make a big fuss about how lucky your toddler is to get one of these gizmos, and she'll be safely snoozing in the crib for many months longer.

If you do decide to take a toddler who sleeps restlessly out of the crib, Dr. Camasto recommends investing in a safety bar that slides under your child's mattress and creates a barrier at the edge of the bed. This gadget doesn't do anything to escape-proof a bed for a toddler who wants to get up, but it does help protect them from falling out. Also, if you're moving a wiggly to a bed, you might consider choosing a "big bed"—with a twin or full-sized mattress—rather than opting for a barely-bigger-than-a-crib-sized toddler bed.

Count caffeine. For some toddlers, diet is a factor in restless sleep. If you think this might be the case at your house, keep a diary of what your toddler eats for three or four days, then take a hard look at how much caffeine he may be ingesting. Caffeine should not be a significant part of any toddler's diet, but it does sometimes hide in the form of sips of soft drinks, chocolate treats, and pre-prepared snacks. I have two nephews who started helping themselves to a little coffee from their parents' mugs when they were still toddlers, fueling themselves up for busy, restless nights. Keep a close eye to see if your toddler is helping herself to any high-caffeine items too.

No wrestling. Trying to get your toddler back to the head of her crib or bed is risky business, because she may wake up at any second and ruin the night for both of you. Don't waste your energy trying to arrange your toddler's sleep position unless you really think she's put herself in danger, says Dr. Camasto. Even if you take the risk, chances are your little one will have changed her position again before your head hits your own pillow.

Ask the doctor. If you believe your toddler's sleep is so restless that it's causing her to wake up without feeling rested and to act tired during the day, give your pediatrician a call to discuss the problem. There are several physical possibilities that may be affecting your toddler's sleep, explains Dr. Camasto. If the doctor confirms your toddler is teething, she may recommend a pain reliever. If the problem is an ear infection, pain meds and/or an antibiotic may solve the problem. In rare cases, your toddler's unusually busy sleep pattern may be related to snoring or to sleep apnea, another treatable condition. Don't let your toddler or the rest of your family suffer if she is chronically overtired. More often than not, toddlers who are consistently overtired can have their sleep disorders diagnosed and treated.

Chapter 31

WHY DO TODDLERS
WAKE UP TERRIFIED?

You may never be more acutely aware of the stages of sleep, the power of the unconscious, or the true terrors of a nightmare until your child is at their mercy. As parents, we spend a huge part of our lives following all the protocols for protecting our offspring: feeding them right, making sure they get enough sleep, buckling them in their car seats, investing in gadgets to protect them from stoves and stairs and scary movies. . . . There are days when we literally don't take our eyes off them for fear that something bad might happen.

But when we tuck our toddlers into bed, we like to think they're out of harm's way. The outlets are capped, the jammies are flame retardant, the reflective firefighter sticker is prominently displayed in the window; it's all been done by the book. When nightmares come charging into that little bit of security in our parenting lives, it seems like a cruel turn. Despite all that we do to protect our children while they're awake, it seems terror can stalk them at will in their sleep.

Scientists have shown that dreaming begins even before birth. Babies and young children, it turns out, spend far more time dreaming than adults. But with cognitive development comes memory, and with memory come the kinds of dreams—and nightmares—that wake toddlers up at night. In fact, some specialists in sleep issues define nightmares as just that: dreams so vivid and unpleasant that they cause the dreamer to wake.

If your toddler wakes up screaming, there's a very good chance a bad dream is the reason. Toddlers under two may not be able to tell you what the problem is, but in the absence of a fever or other physical complaint, a bad dream is your best educated guess, explains Angela Camasto, M.D., a pediatrician in private practice in Easton, Pennsylvania.

If you suspect your toddler has had a nightmare, ask her if she had a bad dream and try to get her to tell you what it was about. It will help her understand that what she dreamed isn't real if you give her the terms to describe it and help her tell you the crux of her fear. Even if all you can get out of her is "Monster," at least you will have your explanation confirmed.

As your toddler gets older, she'll be able to clear any doubt by recounting her nightmares in detail. Studies have shown that as children's ability to imagine and play fantasy games during the day becomes more sophisticated, their dreams can become more vivid, too. Don't be surprised if your nightmaring toddler comes racing to your bed as if there really is something terrible coming up fast behind her—or if your word doesn't cut it when you tell her it was only a dream.

Sometimes it's easier and more effective to work within a child's fantasy to address her fears than to try to convince her they're groundless, explains Marjorie Taylor, Ph.D., professor of psychology at the University of Oregon in Eugene. If your child is convinced there's a witch in the closet or that the shadows are going to get her, you'll gain a lot more ground by going in the closet to investigate or plugging in a nightlight than you will by offering a discourse on the probability of either.

Now That You Know

A dreamy take on reality. There are many times when it doesn't take a psychic to connect the dots between what's going on in your toddler's life and the characters and themes that are populating her bad dreams. A new place, a new person, and a new preschool can all turn up, albeit in slightly scarier form, in your toddler's bad dreams. Do reassure your toddler that the new experiences are safe for her, but don't overreact to her bad dreams. They are another of the many normal, healthy ways toddlers work through the things that intimidate or frighten them until those things aren't so scary anymore.

The season has just begun. It's only fair to note that during the toddler years, the nightmare phase is just ramping up for many children. According to the American Academy of Family Physicians, just 5 to 8 percent of adults have frequent nightmares, while 20 to 40 percent of children suffer with them. The nightmare years usually peak around age six.

Turn off the TV. Toddlers who are watching television are usually calm and quiet, making this seem to many of us like an ideal part of the pre-bedtime, winding down routine. According to research into sleep disorders, though, television is often a factor in keeping kids awake at night. If you are going to allow your toddler to watch TV at night, be very selective. *Bedtime for Big Bird*, for example, might fit just fine into her routine, but if she's keeping you company for whatever is on for adults in prime time you may be exposing her to stimulation from the sounds and images that could keep her up, or cause bad dreams, later.

Beware the feminine imagination. Nightmares are more prevalent among girls than boys, though sleep researchers don't know why.

Don't laugh. The things your toddler has nightmares about may seem cartoonish or even comical to you—after all, if your own nightmares were about a big pink-spotted crocodile chasing you in the grocery store, they wouldn't really be nightmares at all. When your toddler gives you a wide-eyed account of the characters and events that populate his dreams, take them seriously and try to sympathize. If you belittle his fears, he may continue to have the same kind of nightmares—but not feel he has anyone he can tell about them who understands.

When the nightmare is yours. A small percentage of toddlers suffer from a less common sleep disorder called "night terrors." If this happens to your toddler, she may scream or cry as if from a nightmare, but she won't come looking for you. And when you go to her aid, she will seem as if she doesn't know you're there. The strange state of a toddler in a night terror is similar to that of a sleepwalker—a level of consciousness that is stuck between asleep and awake.

If your child suffers from night terrors, your role as a parent is not to console her as it is with nightmares. Your child won't remember anything that happens during the episode. Instead of focusing on comforting her, which may be impossible, you need to ensure that she's safe. In the midst of a night terror, there is no logic to your toddler's actions—not even enough to prevent a bump on the head or a fall down the stairs. The safest course of action is to stay with your child until she slips back off to sleep.

part four

This Little Body of Mine

Chapter 32

WHY DO TODDLERS BITE?

Sometimes in all the excitement of parenting, we forget that our beloved children are, in fact, mammals. They have little to work with in the way of natural defenses, as far as mammals go, but they do have some very sharp teeth.

At some point in their first years, most toddlers try those teeth on a parent, friend, teacher—occasionally even an unsuspecting stranger who gets too close. "You have to remember that toddlers are just beginning to learn self-control," says Megan McClelland, Ph.D., associate professor of human development and family sciences at Oregon State University. "They are easily frustrated. They're just coming out of a period of development where absolutely everything goes in their mouths. When they feel like they need to put on an offense or a defense, they have to use what they've got."

Small wonder they don't bite more often. The reasons for those first bites are wide-ranging. Some toddlers bite when they think their bodies or their belongings are threatened; some bite to get something they want; some use it as a way to release pent-up anger or frustration; many do it just to see what will happen next. What happens next is pretty important in any case of biting, because no parent wants to see a repeat performance anytime soon.

No one approves of biting, but the ways parents address the matter vary greatly. Unlike other behaviors you may be willing to live with while your toddler works his way past them, biting is not one to be handled by looking the other way.

The first thing that needs to happen when your toddler bites is that he is told not to, says Dr. McClelland. Don't waste your breath on a lecture at this point. A simple, firm, low-voiced, "No, we do not bite," will suffice. Don't hit, spank, or shout at your child. Your tone of voice needs to be all business when you're trying to deal with an unacceptable behavior. Next, remove your toddler from the situation. Take him to a corner or out of the room, and tell him "Stay here," or "Time out." If your toddler bit you, put him down if you're holding him; now is not the time to pick him up if you're not.

Give your toddler a few minutes—less than five—of silent treatment, then speak to him in a calm, even voice. Tell him, in as brief a conversation as you can, that you understand that he was feeling upset, unhappy, angry, frustrated—whatever emotion you think fits the situation—but that biting hurts, and that's not what we do when we feel that way.

Sometimes, all it takes is one swift, calm time-out and one explanation to convince a toddler that biting is a bad idea. Sometimes it takes many more tries. In each case, it's important that you don't shower your child with attention—positive or negative—for his indiscretion. He will learn much more quickly to control his own emotions if the response he gets to losing his grip on his temper is predictable, firm, and flat.

NOW THAT YOU KNOW

Be careful what you say. It's the most natural thing in the world for a stressed-out mom to pick up the phone and call her husband, her mother, or her best friend to report that her child has gotten into trouble at Mother's Day Out for biting, again. As Julie plays with pots and pans on the floor, Mom has her conversation. "Julie's so aggressive," she says. "She bit *two* children today. I don't know what we're going to do with her."

The very first thing that Mom needs to do is go cold turkey on talking about her little girl in front of her. You may think that your toddler is too little to understand what you're saying, but language researchers have proven beyond a doubt that children are much more adept at understanding what they hear than we give them credit for. Even an infant can pick out her own name in conversation, and soon after, she can figure out that she's being complained about. Worse yet, some research has shown that very small children can even retain memories of words used to describe them in overheard conversations until they're big enough to know what they mean. It's easy to throw around words like aggressive, troublemaker, and even vicious when you know your toddler can't understand them, but something else entirely if you think they might stick.

Biting is for kids. Anyone who offers you advice on how to curb bad behavior in your toddler means well, but it doesn't mean they know what they're talking about. One popular bit of advice for parents with toddlers who bite is to bite them back. The fact is there is no appropriate moment to bite your toddler. There are lots of better ways to address this problem.

Can you see it coming? If your toddler has started biting, you can help curb the habit by being observant about the circumstances that lead up to each incident. "If your child is biting, head him off at the pass," says Dr. McClelland. "First, validate his anger before he loses it, then give him an alternate way to deal with his feelings." For example, when you see your toddler getting angry, say, "You look like this is making you feel mad. When I'm mad, I like to go run around outside for a few minutes. Let's try that." Another alternative, if your toddler tends to get very angry, is to give him an object he's allowed to take it out on—like an "angry" pillow, or even a makeshift punching bag. (My husband bought a child-sized punching bag for our daughter when she was two and displaying a wicked temper. She rarely hit it, but being reminded that she could seemed to help her get the overwhelming anger under control.)

No good time for this. Everyone involved in raising a child who bites—or one who has been bitten—is in agreement that there is no appropriate time for this habit to develop. That said, though, there is a window of time during which it is developmentally appropriate. Any child under the age of three may go through a biting jag for reasons ranging from trying to get attention to trying to figure out why someone did it to him. Most toddlers pass through this phase within a few months of entering it. If your toddler continues to bite after age three, bring it to the attention of your pediatrician and ask for advice.

Chapter 33

WHY DO TODDLERS CLIMB?

It's amazing what a parent can get used to. My sister and I were standing in her kitchen admiring her new wallpaper when my nephew, then two, strolled in, dragged a step stool from in front of the sink, used it to climb on the garbage can, used *that* to climb on the counter, then strolled across to get himself a cup from the cupboard.

"Lisa?" I asked my sister, trailing the little boy with my arms outstretched, ready to make the big catch.

"He won't fall," she replied. "He loves to climb."

I stepped back and looked again. He did seem pretty solid up there. Apparently this Flying Walenda had been in training for a long time now—so long his mom had forgotten how precarious his routine might seem to an aunt who lives out of town.

There are toddlers who breeze through their early years quite content to stay on level ground. They toddle, then walk, then run—miraculously without ever deciding to scale the furniture or the drapes. There are also children who discover early—often before they can walk—that climbing is a thrill only equaled by the sense of accomplishment they feel when they conquer yet another mountain (or chair, or table, or flight of stairs, or piece of playground equipment).

No one knows for sure why some kids take to climbing and others pass it by, but for most it is probably a mix of a brave, outgoing temperament and early physical coordination that does it, explains Joan Brooks McLane, Ph.D., professor of child development at the Erikson Institute of Child Development in Chicago. An early taste of the advantages of height can be a huge motivator for a child who measures around three feet tall, too.

"Some toddlers are very competent at things we would rather they not learn to do," Dr. McLane explains. "Their parents have to do what they feel comfortable with, what they feel is safe and fair."

For a climber, that level of acceptable activity can be entirely different than for a toddler who stays on the ground.

It usually starts with making sure your climbing toddler can do it without getting into trouble. "Think of yourself as your toddler's first gym teacher," says Dr. McLane, "and make sure he has a chance to practice those skills in a safe environment." Outside climbing time in the yard or at the playground will help cut down on indoor climbing, but some toddlers really need an indoor climbing spot, too. You can make one by stacking up the cushions from the couch or giving your toddler an aerobics step to climb on, but many parents opt for a small climbing center—the kind designed for outside by Fisher Price, Mattel, etc.—to be used indoors. No décor-savvy adult wants one of these behemoths in the house, but consider it a temporary measure, and think how happy your toddler will look on it—much better than he does on the counters.

NOW THAT YOU KNOW

What goes up. First thing first. If your child is climbing, there's no way to stop it completely. At some point, you're going to have to run to the bathroom or to answer the door, and your toddler is going to get stranded high up with no safety net. He needs to know how to get down. Teach your toddler how to sit down, hold on, and back his way off his climbing apparatus by practicing at the playground or in an approved climbing area at home. It may feel strange to be teaching your climber to be better at it, but it'll give your toddler a security blanket he can't get any other way.

Lay the ground rules. The key to keeping your climber happy, safe, and in check is consistency, consistency, consistency. Decide where you will and will not allow climbing, and then help your toddler catch on. Show him where he is allowed to climb. When he starts climbing in any other spot, tell him, "This isn't a good place for climbing! Let's go find a better place." Then take your toddler to the place where he is allowed to climb and play with him there.

Cap the crib. The fact that a toddler can climb out of his crib doesn't necessarily mean you have to take him out of it. Jodi Mindell, Ph.D., a sleep specialist and associate professor of psychology at St. Joseph's University, recommends investing in a crib-topping tent. "Many, many toddlers who are physically capable of climbing out of their cribs are not nearly ready for the challenges of sleeping in a bed," she explains. "This option lets your toddler continue to have the feeling of security the crib held before he could climb out. I highly recommend them." Crib tents are available in department stores and through children's toy and equipment retailers and catalogs.

Chapter 34

WHY DO TODDLERS LOVE TO BE NAKED?

Next time you're at the pediatrician's office, ask to see that developmental milestone growth chart again. Right there under "Age 2" you'll find it: "Takes off clothes." Some of us misguidedly believe that "takes off clothes" is naturally followed by "when asked to," but rest assured, it's not. Your two-year-old will take off her clothes when and where she pleases.

You can put them back on her when you catch her, but streaking toddlers are notoriously fast, and not so easy to grab, either.

"Toddlers are very interested in their bodies and exploring all parts of them," explains Susan Nelson, M.D., assistant professor of family medicine at the University of Memphis Medical School. "Part of their exhibitionist nature comes from being proud of their bodies and a simple desire to be free of restrictions," she explains. "I imagine many adults would gladly shed some of their more restrictive clothing—think ladies' undergarments—if it weren't for the social stigma." But toddlers don't yet live with the burdens of social pressure, and after being taped up in diapers, onesies, and overalls for a year or two, they're very happy to find their smooth, warm, chubby selves underneath.

Further escalating the nudity situation is the fact that toddlers often learn to take their clothes off *months* before they learn how to put them back on. They can strip themselves all day long, but if you want them dressed, you'll have to do it yourself.

Fortunately, most toddlers who are capable of getting themselves out of their clothes are also capable of learning one or two very basic guidelines about clothing. It is possible to let your toddler enjoy her newfound pleasure without making her feel like she's done anything wrong. Tell her, "I'm glad you know how to get your clothes off now, but this is a place where everyone has to be dressed," or "You can take your clothes off in your own room, but not here in the living room." Sometimes giving your toddler a place in the house where nudity is allowed is the best solution to the problem. If she is only allowed to get naked in her own room, you can take her straight there if she decides to strip anywhere else. The move should not be treated as if it's a punishment—just a practical matter that naked people have to be in that room. If you don't laugh or make a big deal about the rule, your toddler will learn to accept it soon.

By the way, don't be surprised to find that your toddler's new fascination with nudity isn't limited to her own body. Many toddlers take a new interest in other people's nudity, too. Because Mom and Dad are such easy targets, it's our nudity that becomes a main focus. Don't be surprised if your toddler pokes her head in the shower door or lingers wide-eyed while you try to get dressed afterward. Don't be shocked or offended if they try to get their hands on your naked parts, either. As uncomfortable as this phase can be for parents, it is a healthy, normal behavior and not an indication of a deviant in the making.

NOW THAT YOU KNOW

Opportunity may be knocking. If your child is two or three and has taken a shine to nudity, you may have a perfect opportunity to work on potty training. A child's ability to take off (and put on) her own clothes is one of the prerequisites for successful potty training, because kids who can't manage to get their own stuff off have a hard time "making it." If your toddler is starting to strip, it may be time to talk about the potty. Many parents who have a hard time helping their toddlers make the leap out of diapers find that naked toddlers are easier to potty train. It's just human nature that toddlers don't like to feel pee running down their legs, and a toilet training process that sometimes takes a few weeks with a child who is comfortably in diapers may be whittled down to a few days for one who doesn't have that cushioning.

If the time has come. If you've decided to give potty training a shot, that should be a factor in how you dress your toddler. For the time being, you're going to have to make it as easy as possible for your toddler to get naked with elastic-waist pants, shirts that do not button underneath, and pajamas without zippers. You may be seeing a lot more of that little streaker if her clothes are even easier to get off, but any embarrassment on your part now will be worth it if your reward is the end of diapering in the immediate future.

If it has not. If it turns out your budding nudist is not ready for toilet training, you may want to err on the side of complicated in your toddler's clothes for a few more weeks or months before trying again. Clothes with buckles, overalls, and shirts that snap at the crotch will all slow your toddler down when she tries to strip at inappropriate places or times. Be sure and allow a time and place, though, when nudity is accepted. Your toddler's interest in self-exploration can be slowed a bit, but you shouldn't try to bring it to a halt.

Don't be offended. Most parents can't help but notice how cute those naked toddlers are. But as a group, we are pretty horrified to see our toddlers, already naked, begin doing things that look suspiciously like masturbation. As surprising as it is, don't overreact. At this age, toddlers' touching of any part of themselves is not a sexual act. They just do what feels good. Since some of their "parts" have been carefully and completely wrapped up for years now, it's not surprising that they give those areas close attention and inspection once they figure out how to get their clothes off.

Chapter 35

WHY DO TODDLERS PICK THEIR NOSES?

It is the inalienable right of toddlers to take a little time during their development to explore all the wonderful nooks and crannies of their bodies. This includes holding their tongues with their hands, picking the crud out from between their toes, manhandling their privates, and poking around in their ears. It's all pretty new and exciting to toddlers, and to some extent, you need to just let them have their fun checking themselves out.

There comes a time in every toddler's personal exploration when his finger finds its way into his nose. It's inevitable. Nostrils are just the right size for little fingers, and if your toddler finds any treasures while he has them in there, he'll be motivated to dig again soon.

The reason, then, that toddlers pick their noses is because they're there.

So parents have to decide what to do about it. Keep in mind as you decide how to address this social challenge that for most kids, it is just a passing phase. If you give it too much attention, your toddler may do it just to ruffle your feathers. Instead of harping on how bad this habit looks or how dirty it is—both issues your toddler couldn't care less about—give him a little help every time you see him picking: get him a tissue. If you consistently deliver a tissue to a toddler picking his nose, along with a straightforward comment like, "This is what we use when we need to touch the inside of our noses," soon the tissue will become part of the habit. It's not a perfect solution, but it will help get you by until your toddler is ready to take the next step.

Eventually, the double-edged sword of peer pressure will undoubtedly bring your child around to the mentality that nose-picking is gross. He may still do it on occasion—as you've probably noticed, many adults do—but at least he'll learn to take the precaution of making sure he doesn't have an audience.

💡 Now That You Know

Stock up on decongestant. Unfortunately, the times when picking a nose is the yuckiest—when there's lots of stuff to pick—are the times when most toddlers kick their picking habits into high gear. That's not surprising. Considering that many toddlers still aren't all that good at blowing their noses, they're finding it hard to breathe. They start snuffling, and *voila,* an investigatory finger goes to work and the picking begins. If your toddler has allergies or persistent colds that clog his nose, you may be seeing quite a bit more of this than the other parents on the block. Using an oral decongestant, nasal saline spray, or a dab of Vaseline on your child's nostrils can all help relieve the stuffiness and dryness that can lead to picking.

It's an easy target. Kids who suck their thumbs seem primed for picking their noses right from the start. The thumb is in the mouth, the rest of the fingers are balled in a fist above it; and right above those is the nose. For most, mercifully, when they give up the thumb, they give up the nose as well.

Busy hands. At some time or another, all toddlers pick their noses. There's nothing particularly neurotic about the habit—*unless* your toddler also bites his nails, constantly fidgets with his hands, and seems unable to ever be still. In that case, nose-picking may just be one more way to occupy his very busy hands. If this sounds like your child, offer something else to keep his hands occupied. Even somethng as simple as a piece of ribbon, a pair of small cars, or plastic animal toys in a bag can help.

Beware of unidentified nasal objects. Just to put things in perspective, note that some parents would be downright grateful to have a toddler who limits himself to putting just his finger in his nose. Angela Camasto, M.D., a pediatrician in private practice in Easton, Pennsylvania has seen a toddler in her office at least once a month with a nasal obstruction. Items that frequently have to be removed in doctor's offices include nuts, raisins, beads, and small toys like Barbie shoes. The more serious cases happen when parents are unaware the object is in there, Dr. Camasto explains. If your child is in the habit of fiddling with his nose and starts to have a foul-smelling nasal drainage, especially from just one side of the nose, there's a good chance the culprit is something that never should have been in his nose in the first place.

A bloody mess. Nosebleeds are often par for the course for toddlers who make a habit of picking their noses. Don't get upset or yell at your toddler for causing a nosebleed—he may well already be terrified at the realization that he is bleeding. Do tell him matter-of-factly that putting his finger in his nose could have caused the problem and help him clean himself up. Unless your toddler becomes listless or pale, is bleeding from both nostrils, or if the nosebleed persists after ten minutes of holding the nose and keeping more-or-less still, there's no need to worry about the health implications of the incident. Nosebleeds are very common and usually harmless.

Chapter 36

WHY DO TODDLERS HOLD THEIR BREATH?

It seems like the ultimate expression of defiance: I will not breathe until things change around here. So there.

As a group, toddlers have many not-so-charming habits that can drive their parents to drink: biting, kicking, screeching, and banging their heads, among other things. But few can intimidate a mom or dad more completely and effectively than a toddler who holds her breath. The coupling of your child's over-the-top anger or frustration with your terror when she begins to turn blue or passes out from the lack of oxygen is most parents' worst nightmare. It's an overwhelming emotional roller coaster of fury, fear, and sympathy. Parents can feel completely bowled over by even the prospect of a child who is willful enough to deprive himself of oxygen until he loses consciousness.

In truth, breath holding is not the deliberate, willful act its reputation implies. If you try, just once, to hold your own breath until you pass out, you'll quickly discover that this isn't something most people can do. While toddlers who hold their breath may indeed be very mad when it happens, for those who are successful at it, it is more of a reflex than a voluntary act. It occurs not just in anger, but also when the child is extremely frightened, or has received a minor injury. The fact that breath-holding often starts in babies as young as six months, and on average in babies at twelve months, also points to the existence of a physiological, not behavioral, explanation. Babies don't know enough about spite and determination to do such a thing on purpose.

Even though toddlers who hold their breath have a reputation among adults everywhere for being little tyrants, behavioral profiles done by Francis DiMario Jr., M.D., associate professor of pediatric neurology at the University of Connecticut, showed no significant differences between the personalities of toddlers who have had breath-holding incidents and those who have not.

Of course, knowing your toddler doesn't do it on purpose doesn't make it any easier to keep your panic in check when your child begins to turn blue or loses consciousness because she's holding her breath. The process may be as hard on your system as it is on your toddler's.

Though you may be sick with worry about a toddler who has a breath-holding problem, rest assured that this is a problem that almost always resolves itself. In a study Dr. DiMario did of ninety-five children who had had this problem, none of them suffered long-term health or emotional problems because of breath-holding, and while most had stopped having incidents by the time they turned five, every last one of them had outgrown it by age seven.

NOW THAT YOU KNOW

Take a deep breath. As unnerving as breath-holding is, it is usually the domain of otherwise healthy, happy children. About a fourth of children have had a breath-holding incident at some point, but about 5 percent have it to the degree that they lose consciousness. Toddlers with this problem are generally unconscious for less than a minute—though it seems like an eternity to anyone looking on. Some children have incidents weekly; others do it daily for a time.

If you have a toddler who holds his breath, one of the hardest things your pediatrician will ever ask you to do is to walk away when your child is having a tantrum and it seems an incident is inevitable. You should keep an eye on your child for her safety, but do not beg her to breathe or threaten her with punishment if she does not; don't punish her or baby her when she comes to. As much as possible, treat each incident as much like a temper tantrum as you possibly can: do what you can to avoid it altogether, give it little attention if it happens anyway, and go on with business as usual when it's over.

Some researchers believe that children who have problems with breath-holding as infants and young toddlers can learn to trigger it in themselves when they're a bit older. If they are correct, it's important that your toddler doesn't learn to use breath-holding incidents—or just the threat of them—as a way to manipulate you.

Offer your support. The fact that the common perception of children who hold their breath is that they are spoiled and willful makes this problem very hard on their parents. If your toddler doesn't do this, but one of her playmates in her family or day care does, you can do your part by making sure you don't pass judgment on the parent or the toddler for the incident. Parents dealing with this situation need all the positive support and understanding they can get.

You can do that—just not here. The biggest immediate danger to children who make a habit of holding their breath is hurting themselves when they pass out. If your child is giving a command performance and it appears she may make herself pass out, be sure she is in a spot where she won't bang her head or fall on anything sharp or particularly hard when she falls. Your reaction to tantrums in the bathtub, on the rock-hard floor of Wal-Mart, or near steps or a balcony should include making sure your toddler has a safe spot to land.

Tell the doctor sooner rather than later. Many of the issues of toddlerhood are best waited out, and breath-holding is almost always one of them. However, because it is a problem that could possibly be confused with several other, more serious medical conditions, it's best to notify your child's pediatrician immediately after a first incident. Many doctors will want to do a one-time check-up, possibly including an MRI, blood work, and other tests to rule out any medical cause for your child's incident. You can expect to be told to take your toddler home and ride this out, but do include the pediatrician in the loop just in case.

A vitamin for this? In the cases of some children, breath-holding has been linked with anemia, and in one small study, taking iron supplements reduced the incidence of breath-holding by over 80 percent. Ask your toddler's pediatrician to test for anemia to see if this might be part of your child's problem.

Chapter 37

WHY DO TODDLERS PEE IN THE TUB?

It is the age-old fraternity prank. Dunk a sleeping buddy's hand in water, and wait to see if he wets himself.

The thing is, the trick wouldn't be "age-old" if it wasn't a sometimes effective means of causing the desired public humiliation. Lest you doubt the medical acumen of boys in college, doctors also acknowledge that bodily contact with warm water stimulates urination: many recommend their patients soak one of their own hands in a warm sink if they need to pee and can't.

If you need proof, just lower your toddler into a bathtub of warm water and see for yourself. The reaction of toddlers to feeling their naked behinds hit a tub of balmy bathwater is almost universal. When a toddler pees in the bathtub, it's just one more bit of evidence that the sophistication and wiring of his nervous system is still under construction, explains Gregory Dean, M.D., a pediatric urologist and associate professor of pediatrics at Temple University. "There are different levels of toilet training—including a long transitional period between not trained at all and fully able to control the impulse to urinate," he explains. "There are some very primitive mammal reflexes that cause the presence of moisture to make a person feel the need to urinate, and it is not until much later in childhood than the toilet training stage that these reflexes can be resisted."

A healthy adult's bladder is regulated by a complex system in which the bladder is constantly relaying messages to the brain about its level of fullness, and the brain continually sends messages back that say, in essence, "not yet." When an adult is ready to empty the bladder, the key messages are transmitted, and a sophisticated series of muscular contractions and relaxations take place at the person's will to get the job done.

Toddlers, of course, fall somewhere in between the baby-on-autopilot system and the adult who can practice such impressive control. Up until age two, they seem oblivious to a full bladder. From there on, toddlers become increasingly able to stay dry for an extended period between urination, and they begin to tune in to how they feel when the bladder is full, and how they feel when they release it. Throughout this phase, however, toddlers continue to be subject to the powers of persuasion of the sound of running water and the relaxation of the bladder that can kick in when they are dunked in the bath.

NOW THAT YOU KNOW

It could be worse. Nobody likes to know a child has peed in the tub, but if your toddler is especially susceptible to it, you may feel better knowing that unless she has a urinary tract infection, her urine is sterile. No one in your family is going to become sick or pick up any kind of infection as a result of a toddler peeing in the bathtub. Rinse your tub as usual or clean it with soap and water before the next bather, and don't let your Mr. Clean side get the best of you.

Put the waterworks to good use. Unless your child is afraid to sit on the toilet, let her sit there for a few minutes while you run her bath. The sound of the running water is likely to stimulate urination while she's sitting on the potty, and give her an early taste of success in toilet training. Don't assume that a toddler who pees in the potty while her bath is being run is ready for toilet training, though, since it may be more of a reflex than an act of will. Consider any pre-bath success a public service for your family, and continue to wait for the traditional signs of toilet training readiness before you ask your toddler for anything else in this area.

Don't get mad. No one in their right mind would chastise an infant for peeing in the tub, but parents sometimes get irritated with toddlers who are at or near the toilet training stage. At least until your toddler can and does willfully empty his bladder before he gets into the tub, don't chastise him for doing so when he gets there. The reaction to the water is a simple, physical reflex (Think about it: when was the last time *you* got in a warm tub without emptying your bladder first?), so treating it like a disciplinary problem doesn't do you or your child any good.

While you don't want to respond with criticism if your toddler pees in the tub, don't treat it like a big joke either. Your toddler *is* going to manage to get control of his urinary tract soon, but if he's been treated like a stand-up comic each time he pees in the tub up until that point, he may continue to do so just to work the crowd.

Bye-bye bubbles. If your older, toilet-trained toddler pees in the bathtub, there's a good chance it's just a momentary slip-up, but if your toddler seems uncomfortable, or if it happens more than once in the course of one bath, it's worth investigating further to make sure there is no evidence of a urinary tract infection. More than twice as many urinary tract infections occur in girls as in boys, so keep in mind that your daughter is at higher risk.

If your toddler has ever been diagnosed with a urinary tract infection, by the way, you should limit her baths to the ingredients of one child and clean water. "Soap, shampoo, perfumes, and bubbles in the bathtub can all cause infections and irritation in little girls," explains Susan Nelson, M.D., professor of family medicine at the University of Memphis Medical School. You can still let your child soak and play in a tub, but save the shampoo for the very end and take her out of the bathwater as soon as it's out of her hair.

Chapter 38

WHY DON'T TODDLERS SEEM TO SMELL THEIR OWN STINKY DIAPERS?

It's amazing that something that looks so good can smell so bad. The average toddler with silky hair, big shining eyes, and cherub body can scare off even the bravest diaper-changing eligible adult with a bad case of stinky pants, and yet carry on playing, chattering, and giving hugs and kisses as if there's not a thing in the world going on back there.

Could it be that they don't know?

Research suggests they might not. In studies done on toddlers up to the age of three, young children pay almost no attention when researchers introduce strong smells—including stinky ones—into the children's play area. Most don't comment and don't investigate the new smells; many don't seem to notice at all. What's more, when toddlers are asked to separate unpleasant smells from nice ones, those under three often can't do it. A smell, as far as they're concerned, is just a smell; like the paint on the wall or the buzz of a ceiling fan, it doesn't rate their attention.

Consider your child's olfactory oblivion as one of the many cues nature gives us as to when toddlers are (and are not) ready to be potty trained. "If a child is not bothered by a stinky diaper, he or she is not ready yet," says Teri Turner, M.D., professor of pediatrics at Baylor College of Medicine.

All of the important cues about toilet training readiness come from the toddler in question, explains Dr. Turner. As strange as it seems that perception of dirty diapers should be a sign your toddler is ready to make the leap and be toilet trained, there are several events that usually happen right around the time a toddler is ready that coincide with that surprising olfactory awakening. "Telling you they have a dirty diaper is one way a child indicates an interest in the process," Dr. Turner says. Other signs include a toddler's strong interest in demonstrating independence and a desire to please you by showing you the things they can do.

"Toilet training is often the first *big* battle parents face with their children," Dr. Turner explains, and it is very much a losing battle for parents who attempt it with a child who is not ready. Toddlers who are pushed too soon feel anger, resentment, and shame. Parents who force the issue often suffer through the same emotions.

You may wonder why your child is still soiling diapers at age two or three when you've heard a hundred times about how you were potty trained—or your mom was—before eighteen months. Your grandma is not lying. In 1957, 60 percent of children in the United States were toilet trained by the time they were eighteen months old—half of those by their first birthday. The difference between what happened with previous generations and what happens now is in the method. Pre-1960s babies—and many in years after—were trained by a method of operant conditioning. Babies who aren't even big enough to climb on and off a toilet can be "trained" to void when they are put on one.

The method works, but takes a long time to accomplish and has a high incidence of accidents and regression. In 1962, pioneering pediatrician and family advocate T. Berry Brazelton introduced the idea of another kind of potty training, one that suggested children should be trained when they are mentally, physically, and emotionally ready—and not sooner. Dr. Brazelton's suggestions struck a chord with millions of parents, and his methods became the new norm. Today, the average toddler is not potty trained until somewhere close to the age of three, and most parents find that children who aren't trained until they're ready become continent quickly and for the long term.

"Parents sometimes forget who the boss in toilet training is," Dr. Turner points out. "It's the child who has control over this process. The keys for parents are patience, perseverance, and keeping your sense of humor. Once you can manage that, it's just a matter of time."

💡 Now That You Know

Getting started. So, your toddler is beginning to notice his odiferous self? Does he also seem to have decided that dirty diapers are uncomfortable and uncool? If so, it's time to provide him with that great toddler status symbol, a potty. Let your toddler sit on his own small potty with and without clothes, in whatever part of the house he likes it best, even outdoors. Don't expect him to put it to good use immediately. As far as your child is concerned, it's going to take a little time to get to know this new accessory.

Dress for success. Once your child starts potty training, all those cute overall sets and tights and even pants with complicated fasteners become a thing of the past. Easy on/easy off clothes will make toilet training easier on your toddler—he's likely to have to run for it with some frequency, and complicated undressing can be the difference between just in time and just too late at this age.

Oh boy! If you think you're spending more time trying to get the potty training thing accomplished with your son than a friend is with a daughter, you're probably right. In some studies of potty training, the boys needed to be reminded four *times* as often as the girls to keep them clean and dry. Don't worry about the lag in boys' potty training too much. It is extremely common, and the boys eventually catch up and start needing to be reminded about other things, like taking care of their dirty clothes and putting the seat down on the toilet, instead.

Start small. Lots of kids who can accomplish toilet training during daylight still need diapers at night. Nighttime dryness can lag several months—sometimes more than a year—behind daytime control, and that delay does not indicate any physical or emotional problem with your child. It's just harder for a small child (with a small bladder) to stay dry for a nine- to twelve-hour night than it is for a three- to four-hour stretch during the day.

Everybody's talking about it. Reading age-appropriate books about potty training—titles ranging from *Bye-Bye, Diapers* to *The Princess and the Potty*—can help get your toddler thinking of toilet training as an accomplishment worth pursuing. If your toddler doesn't want to read about potty training at story time yet, though, don't push the issue. Some toddlers don't want to hear any more about a subject that may already be making them feel pressured.

What's it worth to ya? Although some experts do not recommend rewarding children for successfully using the potty, experienced parents will tell you that a bribe can go a long way to help a child who is *almost* but not quite potty trained make the leap. One child may make a whole day for a trip to Chuck E. Cheese. One will poop in the potty if there's a dollar for his pocket or a star for his reward chart in it for him. Some will do what it takes to get the *Blue's Clues* or Cinderella underwear. If there's a one-time treat you'd like to offer your child in a deal to use the potty, as long as you don't use it to pressure him, there's no reason not to give it a shot. Sometimes that one extra bit of motivation is all it takes to help your toddler decide that he is ready, after all.

Chapter 39

WHY DO TODDLERS POOP IN THE CORNER?

It's often in the unlikeliest of places that your toddler chooses to have her bowel movements. Even the youngest child knows that the bathroom is the spot for this kind of thing, but there she is (mercifully fully dressed and diapered), squatting down under the dining room table, behind the potted plant in the kitchen, or in the corner of your bedroom, filling her pants and acting like she's the only one who knows it.

Toddlers start hunkering down in tucked away places to poop when they start to realize that such matters are private. If your toddler has staked out a particular spot in the house, and if she is using it regularly—often at the same time each day—as a potty place, then she may be ready to learn to poop in the toilet.

Toilet training is a challenge no matter how you look at it, but toilet training for number two is often an entirely separate struggle for both parents and toddlers. While plenty of respected parenting resources tell us to train our toddlers to have bowel movements in the potty *first* (and pee will just naturally follow), those instructions can be much more difficult to follow than expected. The fact is that many toddlers don't mind peeing in the potty at all—it's kind of fun for them, you get all excited about it, and it isn't the least bit uncomfortable. For children who are ready to be potty trained, it often takes just a few tries or a small bribe.

But bowel movements are different, explains Teri Turner, M.D., professor of pediatrics at Baylor College of Medicine. A lot of children worry themselves sick over the prospect of pooping in the potty, for reasons that range from thinking they're going to lose a part of themselves to fearing they're going to be injured from the effort.

A toddler who routinely poops in the corner (or in another spot she's chosen herself) can often make a transition to a toilet more easily than her peers who haven't established a potty habit yet. The trick, says Dr. Turner, is bringing the potty to the toddler.

You may think the bathroom is the only acceptable place for your child to learn to use a potty, but if you have an open mind about the process, you may find things easier for everyone involved if you use that great spot under the dining room table where she has been crouching to have her bowel movements for weeks.

Put a child-sized potty in your toddler's spot, tell her what it's for, and give her some time to think about it. If your toddler is already peeing in a real toilet, this will take less time than if the whole idea is new. If your toddler keeps using the same spot, a little nudity—or at least time spent diaper-free—might be in order. With no diaper on, and the potty waiting in the key spot, most toddlers will opt for the practical solution.

Once a toddler becomes accustomed to using a potty—no matter where it is located—most find it unpleasant to go back to relieving themselves in diapers. When your toddler has established a habit of using the potty in her choice location, it's time to talk with her about relocating it to the bathroom. Chances are very good that given the choices of under the table with no equipment, or in the bathroom with her own private toilet, your child will make the leap to going potty like a big girl.

⚬ NOW THAT YOU KNOW

A special seat for everyone. Whether you are working with your little boy on learning to pee or poop in the potty, for best results, he should start out sitting on the potty. Even though the long-term goal for boys is that they pee standing up, they have an easier time figuring out how to poop in the potty if they learn to urinate there first.

Privacy please. Giving your toddler privacy helps him learn to respect yours. The toddler period is a notoriously, and necessarily, open-door one; after all, part of teaching most toddlers to use the potty is letting them see how you do it. The fact that your child sought a private place to relieve herself, though, means she's ready to give and receive a little more consideration in this area. When your toddler is sitting on the potty, ask her if she'd like you to leave her alone. For some children, potty time is only enjoyable if Mom or Dad hangs out with them to read stories, sing songs, and talk. Others, though, will take you up on your offer and be glad to take care of their business in the bathroom alone.

Smart kid you've got there. Toddlers are often much smarter than we give them credit for, and that intelligence sometimes just naturally leads to manipulation. Each of my children tried to use the "I need privacy" line to get away with doing things they knew they couldn't do while I was watching. While you want to respect your child's newfound sense of herself, you are still going to be well within your bounds for some time to come to simply say, "You really don't need privacy for that," and continue about your business.

Pardon our décor. Some parents are mortified to realize that the key to potty training success is a child-sized toilet in a public part of the house. You can try tucking your toddler's portable potty into the sheltered spot closest to the place she prefers, if you like. Some parents take matters a step further and cut up and decorate a big cardboard box to screen the potty. This trick can actually help matters when you move the potty to the bathroom, because you can take the "wall" you and your toddler made to go around it with you. Regardless of how you approach the decorating challenge the situation poses, keep in mind that anyone who has ever raised a child probably won't even raise an eyebrow. (It's just the young single folks you know who'll be offended.)

part five

In the Mood

Chapter 40

WHY DO TODDLERS THROW TEMPER TANTRUMS?

Toddlers throw tantrums because they want, because they don't want, because they're tired, because they're hungry, because they're sick, scared, worried or just plain mad. Sometimes, it seems they do it because the sky is blue.

No matter how seemingly insignificant the trigger of your toddler's tantrums, don't let anyone tell you she's destined for a life of manipulation and anger because she can't control her emotions when she's one, two, or three. Kicking, screaming, foot-stomping tirades are as much a normal part of toddler development as learning to speak in sentences and eating with a fork. According to Michael Potegal, Ph.D., a neuropsychologist and assistant professor of pediatrics at the University of Minnesota, the majority of children ages one to three have tantrums, and up until around age four, many, many toddlers have them almost every day. "If you come to my office and tell me you have a two-year-old who is having tantrums," says Dr. Potegal, "the most I can diagnose is that your child is indeed two. There may be nothing more to it than that."

If you ask parents what motivates their toddlers' tantrums, the most common answer is that the child is tired. In fact, you may have already noticed that your toddler seems to have tantrum time penciled in on her mental daily planner for any time a nap is held up for any reason, as well as somewhere between naptime and bedtime, usually between 3:30 and 7:30 p.m. Most parents already treat these hours warily, because the so-called witching hour tends to be the most difficult with infants, too.

"The reason we see more tantrums in the late day is not well understood," says Dr. Potegal, "but the fact that more of them take place during that time has been borne out in studies dating back for decades." It may be that as the day wears on, children become less and less capable of dealing with both small aggravations and big ones—like feeling hungry and tired.

"When they're fine and dandy, toddlers can usually withstand some frustration," explains Dr. Potegal. "When they're not, it takes less frustration to kick off a tantrum. In extreme cases, children don't need any frustration at all—they seem primed for a tantrum without any outside stimulus."

Toddlers use their tantrums for many different purposes, ranging from a basic means of conveying anger and frustration to making absolutely certain you understand they *do* want to wear the purple coat and do *not* want to take cough medicine on a given morning. Dr. Potegal points out that the way a parent handles a tantrum should depend on the reason the toddler has thrown it. If the purpose of the outburst is to get something—including your attention—then the most effective course of action is to pay it as little mind as possible. If the purpose is to put off something the toddler doesn't want to do—get in the car or put away toys, for example—then it's important that business go on as usual. In that kind of tantrum, toddlers are meeting their goals every minute they put off the event they are avoiding.

By around the four-year mark, tantrums drop off, both in frequency and in duration. Until then, your job is first to head as many of them as possible off at the pass—and second to make sure the only person who loses her temper over each incident is your toddler.

⚬ Now That You Know

The fewer the better. No matter what you do to prevent them, some tantrums are inevitable. Fortunately, many can be stopped before they start. Keep track of the circumstances that most often aggravate your toddler to tantrum level—some can't stand the stress of shopping, some hate to leave the house, some don't want to eat their vegetables, some can never be late for a nap, some are darned sure not willing to share their toys with their friends and will make sure you know it. Whatever it is that sets your toddler off, try to change the situation or avoid it altogether. For example, if a trip to the grocery store always ends up with your child screaming as you race through the aisles, you have a few choices: find a toddler-free time to shop; change the time of day of your trip; pack a bag of toys and snacks for your toddler to dig through at the store to help her pass the time.

One of your best tools is distraction. If you see a tantrum brewing, change your toddler's location, point of view, or activity. Go outside, point out something your toddler has not yet seen, or propose a new game, toy, or project you can be involved in together. One mother of two daughters, ages two and three, points out that simple phrases like, "Hey, let's color," and, "I guess I'd like to go for a walk," have prevented dozens of tantrums at her house.

From fury to feelings. As your toddler matures, you may be able to intercept a tantrum by encouraging her to talk about her emotions before her temper boils over. Ask her how she feels, and give her the words she needs to express her anger herself. For example, "Do you feel mad because your bear is in Daddy's car? I would be mad if my bear was in Daddy's car, too." Giving your toddler a chance to talk about what is upsetting her can defuse the situation before it's too late.

Hunger plus tired equals tantrum. A hungry, tired toddler is a time-bomb ticking towards a temper event. As you schedule your day, do everything possible to confine errand running and other stressful times to parts of the day when your toddler is fed and rested. If you think you may run into trouble, at least be prepared with a snack—a plastic bag of Goldfish crackers, raisins, or Teddy Grahams can often buy you some time with a toddler who is on the verge of losing her cool.

Your toddler's big show. The truest observation most parents eventually make about temper tantrums is that they are nothing without an audience. Usually, the more effort you put into consoling, cajoling, threatening, or bribing a toddler in mid-tantrum, the longer that tantrum is going to last. Toddlers are quick to note when the adults in their lives fall all over themselves to help them get their tempers under control, and many are capable of generating Oscar-worthy tirades when they're the object of all that attention.

To keep the tantrum to a minimum, don't respond to it. In most cases, you can do this simply by turning your back and refraining from trying to carry on a conversation with your toddler. If you have to leave the room to pull this off, be sure your child is in a childproofed area and not in danger of hurting himself in your absence.

Don't get mad. A big trap parents fall into in dealing with temper tantrums is responding to them with anger of their own, explains Dr. Potegal. In most cases, the parent's anger compounds the child's anger—with the notable and even more undesirable alternative that the adult's anger makes the child feel afraid. Either way, getting mad is the last thing you want to do when your toddler throws a fit. Count to ten, walk out of the room; do whatever you need to do to keep your own temper in check.

Set the tone. The best response to a temper tantrum is to speak in the most matter-of-fact, low, steady, controlled tone you can manage. Dr. Potegal notes that this seems to come more easily to dads, and recommends that moms actually practice their "I'm not fooling" approach ahead of time, looking in the mirror. "You want to look serious without looking furious, and to keep your voice flat," he explains. It is not easy, and it might not shorten the length of the tantrum, but it will keep it from escalating and becoming worse.

Don't be sorry. Most tantrums start with anger and wind down to distress and sadness. "As primates, we are built to respond to unhappiness in other individuals—and that instinct is especially acute in parents and their children," explains Dr. Potegal. It is a very natural inclination to reach out to your emotionally overwrought toddler and try to console her, but it will benefit her most if you can help her get hold of her feelings first. "Tell your child, 'I know that you are upset, and as soon as you stop crying, I'd like to give you a hug,'" says Dr. Potegal.

When push comes to shove. Sometimes the very best thing you can do for a toddler in the midst of a tantrum is to give her a chance to cool off alone. Put your child in her room for a short time, and tell her you'll be happy to spend time with her when she is finished being angry. Your biggest concern during a child's temper tantrum should be that child's safety, so make sure there is nothing she can hurt herself with in her isolation.

How long can this last? No matter what your toddler's tantrum pattern is at ages one to three, do not assume she is going to carry her hot temper into adulthood. It's not until close to age eight—and sometimes older—that the incidence of temper tantrums can be used with any accuracy to predict antisocial behavior in adulthood.

Chapter 41

WHY DO TODDLERS WORSHIP THE GROUND THEIR OLDER SIBLINGS WALK ON?

Why do toddlers gaze up at their older brothers and sisters in starry-eyed admiration? After all, these are people who keep coveted toys out of their reach, interfere with their one-on-one time with Mom and Dad, and get to play during naptime.

In short, toddlers live in awe of their siblings because those big kids have everything a toddler wants. Just look at them. Not only can they walk as if they've been doing it for years, but they can talk in full sentences, sing songs, jump, spin, navigate the playground equipment—*and* they get to play during naptime. Those kids are *amazing*.

Despite their impressive skills set, older siblings are still kids. They're closer in size to toddling brothers and sisters than Mom and Dad, they know how to play, and though they may be too cool for Barney, most still have plenty of shared tastes in everything from toys to movies to favorite foods with younger kids.

"Infants come into this world ready to adore their older siblings," says Laurie Kramer, Ph.D., a professor of applied family studies at the University of Illinois at Urbana whose primary area of research is sibling relationships. "As toddlers, they have endless admiration for older brothers and sisters—kids that are like them, but bigger, stronger, and faster."

"In some ways, we can't really grasp how important sibling relationships are," says DeDe Wohlfarth, Psy.D., assistant professor of psychology at Spalding University. "Siblings are more genetically alike than any other human beings on earth except identical twins, and they share the same environment from the day the younger child is born. Those connections, regardless of whether siblings grow up to be best friends or have strained relationships, are forever."

The implications of having siblings—both older ones and younger ones—are wide-ranging for toddlers. They include everything from having a wonderful built-in playmate to having to deal with the ravages of jealousy and competition very early in life. For most, though, a brother or sister offers great rewards. "Toddlers learn to form relationships with other people by interacting with their siblings," explains Dr. Kramer. They begin to understand how to play cooperatively and to be aware of other people's feelings. One of the biggest benefits for toddlers comes from the fact that sibling relationships give them a relatively safe place to make social mistakes. Dr. Kramer points out that brothers and sisters, unlike most playmates, are your toddler's for life. Your little one can feel anger or frustration or jealousy towards a sibling with the full security that he'll be forgiven and loved all the same before long. Whether you're two, twenty or sixty-five, friends like that are hard to find.

NOW THAT YOU KNOW

Not my job, Mom. If you want to foster a positive, loving relationship between siblings, try not to make them responsible for one another, says Dr. Wohlfarth. Big kids who are held accountable for the actions of their little brothers and sisters soon get sick of them. It's fine to ask an older child to check on or play with or help a younger child sometimes, but it should always be a request, not a demand.

Something in common. Regardless of the age difference between your children, there are always a few activities they can enjoy together. Don't assume they can't or won't play together, says Dr. Kramer. "Parents tend to jump in and tell an older child that a game is too hard or too rough for a toddler, but unless there is a physical danger to the younger child, let them play. Things like playing outside in the sandbox or kicking a ball or make-believe play can all be enjoyed together by siblings with years between them." If they find ways to enjoy each other's company, the time together will strengthen the bond between them.

Lost without you. In a laboratory study in which toddlers were given identical t-shirts and asked to identify which one belonged to their sibling, the majority could pick out the shirt their brother or sister had worn. They recognized the way it smelled. The study was one on olfactory ability, but it also shed a little light on how deeply connected toddlers are to their siblings.

Some toddlers experience the same kind of separation anxiety they feel when their parents have to leave when they must get along without a sibling who has gone off to school or Grandma's house without them. According to Dr. Wohlfarth, the best antidote is to set aside time to do something special with your toddler while his sibling is gone—especially if the older child's absence is a new experience for your little guy. Plan a trip to the park, pack a picnic, or watch a favorite movie with your toddler, but give him a little more of your time and attention than usual to help him cope with suddenly being left alone.

Keeping the peace. Fights between siblings are inevitable, but the way you handle them can help keep them to a minimum or let them take over your children's relationship. A lot of well-meaning advisors will tell you to let your kids work out their differences between themselves, but Dr. Kramer's research has found that for children younger than age eight, this rarely works. "Young children don't have the problem-solving skills they need to work out their own disagreements," she explains. As a result, what begins as a dispute over a toy can rapidly escalate into a screaming, hair-pulling, knock-down battle if you're not careful.

The answer to most children's battles is neither looking the other way nor just jumping in to dispense justice. Try to help your children come to a solution to their problems together. Let each child tell the other how he feels, and let them suggest ways they can resolve their problem. Early lessons in peacefully working out their differences will be invaluable in your children's relationships with their peers (and co-workers) later in life.

When your toddler is the big kid. According to Dr. Kramer, the best thing you can do for your toddler as he welcomes a new sibling is to be truthful about the changes to come. It's fine to talk with an older child about what fun a baby will be and how much the family will love him, but be sure you also prepare your toddler for the fact that the baby will need some of your time, and that the baby won't do much but sleep and eat for a while after she comes home. Oftentimes, toddlers get the mistaken impression that a new baby will be something akin to a new toy. Let your child know from the beginning that a baby is a separate person with needs and feelings of its own.

Separate, not equal. As parents, we do our best to be fair. Sometimes that means pouring the juice in two cups to precisely the same height, and sometimes it means very sophisticated juggling of the different emotional priorities and needs of different children. In Dr. Kramer's research, she has found that siblings with good relationships often share one common, and unexpected, bit of knowledge. They know that "fair" doesn't always mean "equal." "It's extremely difficult for parents to make sure that everything is even," Dr. Kramer explains. "And in trying to make it that way, you're setting yourself up for failure." Instead, try to teach your children from a very young age that everyone in the family gets what they need. "On the most basic level, it means that when your child says, 'He got more M&Ms,' you don't argue the point, but ask him if he's still hungry," says Dr. Kramer. "But on another level, it means that the individual characteristics and needs of each of your children are recognized." They must realize that when one family member needs more time or attention—or M&Ms—on a particular day, that doesn't change the fact that you have enough love for all of them.

Chapter 42

WHY DO TODDLERS TELL LIES?

So your toddler says a pink elephant made that mess in his room, and a cousin who lives three hundred miles away is the one who really peed in his pants. Congratulations. This is proof positive your child has figured out that who he is and what he thinks are not one and the same as who you are and what you think—a significant cognitive leap.

If you are hearing those first fibs before your child turns three, you might also like to know that your toddler may be more intellectually advanced than most of his peers, something that may turn up later in IQ tests. Research shows that children who start lying early have figured out something that almost every child figures out eventually: a lie can keep you out of trouble—when you mess up your room, wet the bed, or bonk your sister on the head, among other inconvenient occasions. When three-year-olds are tested to see if they will lie, about half do so, explains Kang Lee, Ph.D., an associate professor of psychology at the University of California at San Diego who has researched children's truthfulness in the U.S. and abroad. By four or five, they all do it.

Those first fibs, unlike the ones that will come later on, are pretty innocent—and hopelessly unconvincing. While your toddler is indeed tinkering with the facts, he doesn't know a lot yet about deception. He doesn't understand that what he says and what you believe may not be one and the same. He makes no effort to come up with a likely story, let alone one he can really sell with his delivery.

It often happens that by the time your toddler has repeated a particular fib a few times, he's convinced himself (though not anyone else) that it's true.

If you can picture the development of your toddler's brain, you can get a better appreciation of why, so soon after he begins to talk, he starts tossing around untruths like a seasoned politician.

Every toddler's brain is a work still in progress, with mental connections being made at an astonishing rate during every day of this stage. At first, those connections are filling up the right and left hemispheres of his brain, making leaps like the ones from crawling to walking and from single word statements to complete sentences possible. Later in the toddler stage, though, the development of a part of the brain called the prefrontal cortex kicks in. This is the segment of the brain believed to contain centers of moral behavior. Scientists believe the ability to tell right from wrong, to interpret and respond appropriately to social situations, to understand rules, to imagine how other people think and feel, and to inhibit one's own behavior are all tied into the prefrontal cortex's function.

As your toddler's frontal lobes mature, it's inevitable that he'll begin to think about and experiment with telling lies and stories to see how they are perceived. Since this is a milestone every child eventually comes to, it's really not the fact that it happens that matters, but what comes next.

NOW THAT YOU KNOW

Listen to your budding storyteller. There's a difference between the tales your toddler tells you in hopes of avoiding trouble (the "It wasn't me" variety) and the ones that come from other motivations. If your toddler tells you the pink elephant came into the yard and ate the blue turtle and then he had to get his sword and battle it to the death, his intention is to engage and entertain—but not to deceive. Instead of raining on his parade by trying to bring him around to admitting his story is all fiction, ask him questions about his fantasy, and let him tell you more. Putting fantasies into words is tough language homework for a toddler, but if the topic is all his, he'll throw himself into the job. As a culture, we don't accuse fiction authors of lying, and we shouldn't take that view with creative toddlers, either.

Don't try to fight it. Having a heart to heart with your toddler about the shamefulness and moral weakness of lying is about as good a use of your time as talking quantum physics with him. He just doesn't have the mental capacity to make that distinction yet. Don't call him a liar, or tell him he'll be punished if it happens again. You'll have plenty of time for those approaches when he gets a little older. For the time being, calmly tell your child that you know what you are hearing is not true, then ask your toddler to do whatever you have in mind to correct the transgression. For example: "I know you hit your sister, and she is hurt. I need you to go tell her you are sorry," or "I'm sure that you are the person who dumped the dog biscuits. Now let's clean them up together."

When the truth comes out. If your toddler does fess up after telling a fib, praise him for his honesty—and don't punish him for whatever he did that made him decide to lie in the first place. If you reinforce toddlers for telling the truth, consistently and starting when they are young, says Dr. Lee, you may have fewer problems with them telling lies as they get older.

Keep your expectations real. Even at the very innocent age of two, toddlers get a pretty good feel for the way their families feel about them. They thrive on love, but they can get uptight if they sense they are being put on a pedestal by unrealistic expectations. Let your toddler know that you accept him as he is—by complimenting him, by interacting with him, by letting him pursue the things that interest him most—and make sure he knows that even grown-ups spill milk and break stuff from time to time. If nobody expects a child to be perfect, he's not going to be as uptight about making sure to cover his tracks the next time he does something wrong.

Choose punishments with care. While the percentage of children who tell lies holds steady in the general population all over the world, there is one group parents should know always figure it out first. "When we have tested a group of three-year-olds who attend a school in another culture where they are subjected to corporal punishment," explains Dr. Lee, "the number of subjects who lie rises to close to 100 percent, and in general, those children are very good at it, too." Corporal punishment at home can have the same effect, a result that may not be all that surprising. If the punishment a child might avoid by telling a lie is severe, they're more likely to reach the milestone of telling one sooner.

Chapter 43

WHY DO TODDLERS COOPERATE IN SLOW MOTION?

If there is one privilege of early childhood I covet as an adult, it's a toddler's right to exist in her own, self-regulated perception of time. Within the bounds of their parent-controlled schedules, toddlers have the luxury of following their fascinations, sometimes racing at breakneck speed from one experience to the next; sometimes lingering over one toy, one concept, one new skill for hours, or even days.

It is a wonderful, peaceful way to get to know the world.

What a shame that adjusting to living on toddler time once you're grown is enough to drive many a clock-watching adult off the deep end. If you're not careful, all the beauty in the way a toddler coasts through time can be lost in the flurry of "Hurry up and get your shoes," "Hurry up and put that away," "Hurry up and finish your sandwich," and other statements that swirl around her.

"Parents can have a great deal of difficulty adjusting to how much time goes into just getting through simple, routine things with a toddler," says DeDe Wohlfarth, Psy.D., assistant professor of psychology at Spalding University. A quick trip to the market can turn into a full morning's ordeal; a simple shower for your child (and the requisite wrestling on of the pajamas that follows) can take every minute between dinner and bedtime. In a culture where we put a lot of emphasis on what we have to show for our efforts, parenting a toddler can make even the most devoted parent feel like her life has become a long series of asking, preparing, cajoling, and begging her child through matters that were once so simple and routine they didn't even make the To Do list.

Enlisting your toddler's cooperation in keeping the family's schedule in sync is a delicate matter. You have both a right and an obligation to ease your child into the rhythms of everyday life that make things run smoothly for school-aged kids and for adults, but most of us also realize that our toddlers are creating their own mental, cognitive, and social advances quite efficiently on toddler time, and we'd be wise to give them some latitude to do so.

For many parents, trading off blocks of time between the two diverse approaches to getting things done is the secret. "Your toddler needs to have both scheduled and unscheduled time every day," explains Dr. Wohlfarth. Scheduled events should include a waking, dressing, mealtime, naptime, and bedtime. Undoubtedly, there are non-negotiable events you need to work in, too. For at least two substantial blocks of time each day, though, your toddler should be able to play and explore within his own freewheeling concept of "time management"—a guideline that holds true for child care schedules, too.

For many toddlers, transition times are trying times. Some throw tantrums almost exclusively during their transitions from one activity to the next. They seem to have difficulty getting out of one mode and into another—especially when they're going from a fun or unstructured activity to a more practical one. If your toddler dawdles and drags his feet when it's time to get from point A to point B, follow the suggestions here to try to speed things up.

NOW THAT YOU KNOW

Save the names. Do you really want your toddler to know what lazy means? Probably not. Try to resist the temptation to refer to your child as a "lazybones" or even a "poky puppy" when she's slowing you down. It's easy for behavior labels to backfire at this age; your toddler may very well identify with the label and drag her feet even more when she hears it.

Sound the warning bell. For many toddlers, the worst thing that can happen is to be abruptly dragged from what they're doing. Make a point of giving your toddler a five-minute warning, even though she can't tell time, and stick to your plan when the five minutes is up. The precision of the time-left measurement isn't the issue for your toddler; it's the warning, followed by the predicted event. After you've gone through the routine a few times, your toddler will accept that five minutes really does mean a change of scene coming up soon. The time between the warning and the event gives her a chance to get used to the idea before she has to actually do anything about it.

Did you get that? Sometimes mixed signals and unrealistic expectations set parents and their toddlers up for big problems as they transition from one activity to the next. You have every right to ask your toddler to take some small role in ending one activity or beginning the next. At this age, though, don't set yourself up for conflict by asking too much. Give your toddler a single task—she is only capable of keeping track of one goal at this stage. When you give your instruction, no matter how wrapped up you are with the business at hand, slow down, look your toddler in the eye, speak clearly, and keep your instructions as short and simple as possible.

A race to the finish. There are times when nothing but faster will do. If you're late or in a hurry, instead of hustling your toddler with pleas or threats, lay down a challenge. Racing against your toddler (and letting him win) or pitting him against an egg timer or stopwatch can make the difference between on time and not even close. If your toddler is especially receptive to this kind of game, you might decide to make it a part of your daily routine. For example, you can time your toddler each night as she gets her clothes off at bedtime, keeping track of each time she "beats her record" on a sticker chart on the wall.

Chapter 44

WHY DO TODDLERS FAVOR ONE PARENT (AND THEN THE OTHER)?

"I made this for you, Mommy!" Connor shouted when we opened his backpack from preschool and took out the sheet of construction paper covered in red, blue, green, and yellow handprints. I started to tell him how much I loved it, but then my husband walked in.

"I mean, no, not for you," Connor hastily corrected himself, turning his back to me, artwork in hand. "I made this for *you*, Daddy!"

Ouch.

If you've ever been wounded by the swift rejection of a toddler, know that at least you're in good company. Every parent falls out of favor from time to time, and some of us feel like we get the cold shoulder more often than could possibly be fair.

The fleeting affection of toddlers is a normal, healthy part of their development—and not any indication that your toddler doesn't need or love you, explains Laurie Kramer, Ph.D., a professor of applied family studies at the University of Illinois at Urbana.

In fact, it's usually toddlers who do feel secure who are willing to push their parents' buttons by turning their affections on and off. One of our main responsibilities as parents is to help our kids feel secure and attached to us, something we accomplish in the first year by cuddling, feeding, talking to, and comforting our babies. After we successfully establish that attachment, though, it becomes the toddler's job to test it. If you pay close attention, you may be able to see the streak of "Will you still love me if I . . ." when your toddler chooses to play favorites between his parents.

In some families, this division of affection goes beyond Mom and Dad. While most of us can live with the fact that our toddlers will drop us like a hot potato if Grandma or Grandpa is around, it's harder to take when your toddler shows a preference for a child care provider. This common situation plays on any worries a working parent has about day care, but there is little reason for insecurity. Several studies have been conducted to investigate the level of attachment infants and toddlers have toward their child care providers versus those with their parents. In the case of toddlers, the results are always the same: toddlers are more securely attached to Mom and Dad.

🔆 NOW THAT YOU KNOW

Put your game face on. A toddler's rejection can feel like a shot to the heart, but as the grown-up, you've got to take it in stride. The most important thing about your reaction to your toddler's brush-off is that you don't make him feel rejected in return. It's fine to show disappointment at not being the favorite parent of the moment, but your toddler needs to know your love is unconditional. Accept his favoritism gracefully and make sure he knows his cold shoulder is not near enough to make you stop loving him.

If you are the primary caregiver. Stay-at-home moms and dads enjoy many of the privileges of parenthood: they're there for the first steps, the first words, and the day-to-day joys (and trials) of raising a child. When you're with your toddler every single day, though, you'll sometimes find that your presence is taken for granted. In my stay-at-home years, there were times when I was pretty sure my toddlers couldn't distinguish me from the wallpaper.

As disappointing as it may feel to get this treatment, remind yourself that you have the lion's share of your toddler's time. If you need reassurance that your little one enjoys your company, set aside a time for just the two of you to do something special and out of the ordinary. A trip to a playground or a zoo, or even just an hour spent playing on the floor with a box of blocks or Play-Doh, will remind you and your toddler how much you enjoy each other's company.

If you don't have a lot of time at home. If you're a parent who works long hours, spends a lot of time on the road, or shares custodial rights, it can be harder to accept your child's favoritism without worrying it might have a more significant meaning. There are several things you can do to help solidify your position with your toddler when you have a limited amount of time together:

- *Give your toddler your full attention when you're spending time with him.* If he's reluctant to come to you, start an activity you know he'd enjoy without him, look like you're having a good time, and see if he'll join in.

- *Join in your toddler's routine in a predictable way whenever you can.* For example, you may not be able to be with your child for bedtime every night, but when you are, always participate in the same way. Try helping to pick up the toys in his room, making up a silly song, or reading a special story. Choose something that is uniquely yours to share with your toddler and let him know that he can count on that when you are with him.

- *Don't expect a hero's welcome.* For reasons only they understand, many toddlers won't give the time of day to a parent who has just walked in from a long day—or a long week—away from home. Your child has no idea an "I missed you" is what you're hoping for. Don't let a chilly reception when you come home set the tone for the rest of the day. Instead, expect your toddler to take a little time to warm up to you again. If you get that big welcoming hug, it'll be a pleasant surprise.

Set the example. Your toddler makes an art form of studying and mimicking the way his parents interact with one another and with others. If he is reticent about spending time or cuddling with the other parent, make sure you aren't feeding those feelings by treating that person coolly. If your toddler can see that you trust and like the parent he's on the outs with, it'll be much easier for him to do the same.

A little gratitude may be in order. As hard as it may be to feel even a little bit of rejection from your toddler, unless you're constantly in the doghouse with him, try to take the times when he wants someone other than you as an opportunity to do something for yourself. When the other parent is the object of your toddler's affection, make yourself a cup of coffee, spend a little time reading a book, or just be glad for a chance to catch up on the laundry. Raising a child is much more than any day or week when you're not the favorite. No doubt, your toddler will be swinging your way again soon.

Chapter 45

WHY DO TODDLERS SUFFER FROM SEPARATION ANXIETY?

We all know separation anxiety as a kind of toddler affliction—not quite a disease, but close. One day, you can walk away without fanfare. The next, there is leg-clinging and screaming and mournful cries of "Mooommmy" ringing in your ears. It's nice to be loved, but it's awful to feel the guilt and worry that come with having to walk away from a child who seems to think she can't survive without you. What have we done to turn our children from wonderful, well-adjusted babies to toddlers who take every parting so very hard?

The truth is, separation anxiety is not about what you have or haven't done to make your child needy and afraid. It's God's way of making sure your toddler gets through his personal age of exploration in one piece. It's natural to think that something you—or someone else—did or said led your toddler to suddenly become a clingy wreck, but research suggests that a phase of separation anxiety is nearly as normal, healthy, and par for the course as teething.

"Separation anxiety is a very healthy adaptation in infants and toddlers that kicks in around the time they become able to take off on their own," explains Mark Strauss, Ph.D., Director of the University of Pittsburgh Infant and Toddler Center. "It's easier to understand if you think of the way the world would be if we were not living in nice, safe, baby-proofed houses, but in a more wild and uncontrolled environment." At the age when our young can first wander away and put themselves in the line of danger, Mother Nature instills them with a healthy fear of doing so. In fact, researchers have observed the very same behavior at the same stage of development in other primates, reinforcing the idea that it is a normal, adaptive part of growing up.

Officially, studies show that separation anxiety peaks at around fifteen months of age, but a related—and to parents often indistinguishable—behavior known as separation protest can go on for much longer, sometimes until a child is school age.

In an often-cited study, researchers put young children on a tabletop which was solid, but which had a clear outer rim that made it appear to drop off. The infants in the group were equally inclined to roll on the solid portion of the table and the clear section. They showed no hesitation or concern for their own safety. Older infants and toddlers, though, were not so brave or so foolish. When faced with the scary side of the table, they inevitably looked to their mothers for reassurance. The vast majority of those whose mothers smiled and encouraged them to come crossed. Those whose moms looked afraid stopped in their tracks and did not proceed.

"Toddlers draw toward their parents in the face of new settings and new people as a source of self-protection," explains Dr. Strauss. "They use their parents as a kind of safe 'home base,' venturing out a little bit, then checking back. It's quite natural that they would be unhappy to see that safe base walking away. As they become more able to adapt and look out for themselves, they'll be less and less afraid of separation."

One day soon, your child will be able to dive into new situations without looking back, and it may turn out that the one with long-term separation issues isn't her at all—it's you.

💡 NOW THAT YOU KNOW

Hey, who wouldn't be worried? First and foremost, don't leave your toddler with an unfamiliar person or in an unfamiliar place, says Ellen Hock, Ph.D., professor of human development at Ohio State University in Columbus. It is genuinely traumatic for your child to suddenly find herself alone with a stranger or in an unfamiliar place, and that is a reasonable fear. If you will be leaving your child with a babysitter, have the sitter come to your house on a couple occasions during which you do not leave before you expect your toddler to stay with that person alone. If you are enrolling your child in a daycare or preschool, ask the director and teachers if you can stay the first day or two with your child. Allowing some time for familiarity to develop can go a long way toward helping a toddler adjust to new people and places.

Finding the right fit. Not all adults hit it off with new neighbors, employers, or potential friends, and not every qualified caregiver is going to be a good match for your toddler. If there is one sitter your toddler truly doesn't like and can't settle in with, trust your child's judgment and find someone else. If your toddler just doesn't want to be left with anyone but you, that's another issue entirely.

The master plan. Easing your child's separation anxiety starts with a well-planned exit and return. "Have all your things ready, and clue in your babysitter or teacher about how you are going to make your exit ahead of time," says Dr. Hock. "When you are ready to leave, lean down, tell the child that you are leaving, and tell him or her when you will be back. If your child can look at a clock or watch while you are gone, better yet, but make it very clear that you will be back.

"Tell your child you want her to stay with the care provider, that she will be safe and have fun with that person. At that point, the babysitter or teacher should step in and take the child's hand, and you should leave quickly, saying 'good-bye,' and 'I will be back.' The longer you drag out your departure, says Dr. Hock, the harder it will be on you and your child. Go ahead and leave, and be sure to return on time for the happy reunion. If things have gone well while you were gone, you may find that your child is reluctant to leave her new friend at pick-up time.

Timing is everything. When your toddler is struggling with separation each time you leave, it may help to keep those departures on a regular schedule. "Some children have an easier time with separation if they know when to expect it," explains Dr. Hock.

Look at the long term. For some toddlers—estimates range from 10 to 20 percent—separation anxiety is just a fact of life. These are the children for whom moms have quit their jobs, daycare centers have rewritten their rule books, and grandmas have done everything humanly possible to accommodate by taking on babysitting duties themselves. If your child does not respond to a regular schedule with a loving, trusted caregiver after a few weeks' trial time, yours may be one of these. There is no quick fix to overhaul a child's personality—and you undoubtedly wouldn't want to if you could. If there's a way to give your child more of your time—or that of a caregiver the child prefers—during the toddler and preschool years, even the child who cries "Don't leave" loudest at two can be capable of a curt "Bye, Mom" by the time she gets to school at five.

Chapter 46

WHY DO TODDLERS WHINE?

The toddler years aren't quite complete without a little whining. Part of mastering the infinite intricacies of language is experimenting with different tones, and learning language is one of the more substantial tasks laid out for your child between ages one and three. As a dutiful student, your toddler is going to try his hand at everything from a whisper to a squeal, and from a roar to a whine.

The whine, by the way, may well stay in his repertoire for a lifetime.

The reason toddlers whine is sometimes that they stumble on it all on their own, but more often that they hear someone else doing it. Siblings can be the culprits, but friends, teachers, and parents can set the example, too. (If you think you never whine, try to remember the last conversation you had with your spouse after staying up half the night while he—or she—slept like a baby. Who *was* that whiny person?)

What happens in your home once your toddler decides to give whining a try can impact his linguistic and social development for some time to come. If your toddler whines and you teach him that it's really not his most effective mode of communication, he'll learn to use it only for special occasions and extenuating circumstances. If he whines and you respond by showing him you'll do anything to make it stop, well, toddlers may be immature, but they're not stupid. He's going to work his new discovery for all it's worth.

Parents, indeed society in general, are divided about how much whining in a complaint mode is too much. For some of us, even a little makes the hair stand up on the backs of our necks, much like fingernails on a chalkboard. For others, it's a fair way to talk about things that anger or upset us—at least in small doses. Most melt with pity when our toddlers use it to convey that they don't feel well or that they miss Grandpa.

We all pretty much agree, though, that toddlers' whining to convince someone to get them a cup of juice, to turn on *Dora the Explorer,* or to wrangle a few more minutes before bedtime is wholly unacceptable.

"The best way to stop manipulative whining is to address it as soon as it starts and be consistent in your response," says Megan McClelland, Ph.D., associate professor of human development and family sciences at Oregon State University. "The first thing you need to do is resolve not to give in."

Whether you decide to tune out whining, or to address it every time, be sure you, your spouse, and any other caregivers for your toddler are all in agreement about how you're going to deal with whining (or any other behavioral problem, for that matter). If whining is working for your child anywhere, he's going to keep coming back with it until that success stops.

When you deal with whining in your toddler, keep in mind that an occasional self-pitying, tortured, woe-is-me whine is one of the inalienable rights of people of all ages. You're not trying to eradicate it completely, just keep it from taking over your life.

NOW THAT YOU KNOW

Parlez-vous **without the whine?** Perhaps the simplest way to teach your toddler not to whine is not to respond to it. It's not fair to ignore what your child is saying, but very reasonable to tell her you can't understand because of her tone of voice. Toddlers can follow your logic from a very young age when you tell them you can't understand what they are saying. Don't tell them they are whining; the vast majority will change their tone of voice when they repeat themselves without even thinking about it.

Right back atcha. As tempting as it is to mimic your child's whining to show him how terrible it sounds, don't give in. It may hurt your toddler's feelings or make him mad; it may also amuse him to hear you trying to sound the way he does. Either way, it won't solve the problem. When your toddler is a little older, by the way, you may very well be able to use your own comical whine to make him think about how he sounds, but at this age, he's just too young to appreciate the irony.

A small step. It's a very small leap for most toddlers from a whine to a tantrum, so it's important to take care that your standoff with your toddler over tone of voice doesn't turn into a battle of screaming, kicking, and crying, too. If you see that your toddler's temper is escalating, don't give in, but do try to create a distraction or change the subject before things get out of hand.

Funny you should try that. When toddlers are whining because they're angry, jealous, or overtired, it's not a great time to jump in and try to make them laugh. If your toddler is just starting to whine, though, or not quite emotionally spooled up yet, sometimes a little levity goes a long way. You might ask your toddler, "What *is* that terrible sound coming out of your mouth? Can I just look and see if there's something in there? Oh, my goodness, it's a squeak. I think I've got it. Can you talk in a normal voice now? Let's see. Say something!"

Friends don't let friends whine. It's true that whining often drops off significantly when children head off to school. Whining, after all, is about as uncool as it gets. Unfortunately, just waiting out this behavior until that time is not very effective. Your child may swear off whining when he gets to first grade or so at school, and he probably won't do it when friends are over, but if he's in the habit of whining to Mom and Dad, he's likely to keep doing it, a little more privately, forever.

Chapter 47

WHY DO TODDLERS CLING TO PACIFIERS AND THUMBS?

If there's a moment that sweeps you back to the infant your toddler was, it's peeking in on her at night and discovering that she's still sleeping with her limbs tucked up under her like a turtle, thumb in her mouth, back rising and falling in deep, even slumber. She's not so big after all.

Unfortunately, the thumb—or pacifier—that reminds you of those first months at night can be a source of stress and anxiety during the day. Pacifiers get dirty, get lost, and get disapproving stares from strangers and critical comments from relatives. Thumbs don't get lost, but they do get dirty, get dirty looks, and become red, sore, and irritated from the workouts they're subjected to.

Toddlers cling to what pediatricians and dentists refer to as "non-nutritive sucking" because they've learned to comfort themselves by doing so, explains Teri Turner, M.D., professor of pediatrics at Baylor College of Medicine. What began as an infant's instinct to suckle to meet her caloric needs somewhere along the way became the need to suck to feel comforted—not a very big leap, really, for a baby. In some ways, it's a good thing: an immature soul who has already figured out a way to make herself feel better when she's scared, tired, or overstimulated. Being able to do that without the help and handling of a parent is a social advantage. But in a society that often openly frowns on toddlers' need to suck, it's also a disadvantage.

For toddlers under two, even the majority of orthodontists and dentists—the most vocal critics of nonnutritive sucking—say a toddler's jaw is very forgiving. After age two, some point out that your toddler may begin to develop an overbite. Other medical professionals—including many in the dental field—are much more tolerant. Many pediatricians recommend leaving the habit alone until the toddler is significantly older. "It tends not to be too much of a medical issue until they are around the age of five," says Dr. Turner. "That's when we really begin to worry about its effect on the teeth. That's also when a child can begin to actively cooperate to eliminate the habit."

In the meantime, don't draw any more attention to your toddler's habit than you have to. Avoid lecturing about it or discussing it with your spouse or other people in front of your toddler. If there is one universal truth about toddlers who suck their thumbs or pacifiers to soothe themselves, it is that the bigger deal you make about that habit, the harder it is likely to be to break. Trying to force the issue before your child is ready—especially if it's her thumb and not a pacifier—is going to be a losing battle. In many cases, because it's a battle over the activity that makes your toddler feel safe and comforted, it's a battle that may leave her feeling insecure.

The best thing to do about a toddler who relies on a thumb or pacifier is very little. According to the American Academy of Pediatric Dentistry, the number of children who are still using a pacifier or sucking their thumbs whittles down to about 20 percent by age three. In the remaining two years before formal schooling starts, the vast majority of that 20 percent also decide to give up their habit.

NOW THAT YOU KNOW

Let's trade. Some parents successfully ease an attachment object into their toddlers' lives as a substitute for a pacifier or thumb, says Dr.

Turner. It might be a blanket or a stuffed animal, offered to your child when you know she's going to be looking for her binky or engaging her thumb. This is a slow transition, with your child using both the snuggly object *and* the sucking object for a time, but some children are able to ease over to just relying on the substitute for comfort. Since your toddler will be using the snuggly at night, be sure it doesn't have any parts that could be choking hazards.

Don't trade for food. Some parents also successfully ease the concept of comfort food into toddlers' lives by substituting treats for the pacifier, or offering food rewards for abstaining from the thumb. In the long run, your toddler is probably much better off having an oral fixation than having unhealthy eating habits, so it's best to keep food out of the issue altogether.

For pacifiers only. The advantage of pacifiers over thumbs is that thumbs are ever-present. Many parents are able to negotiate with their toddlers to put the pacifier away for limited times during the day—for example, you can tell your toddler that the binky belongs in the crib or bed, and she'll have it there when she goes back for naptime and bedtime.

Not just any pacifier. If your toddler is bound and determined to keep her pacifier, you don't have to press the issue just yet. Make sure, though, that the one she uses is not going to do permanent orthodontic damage. Choose pacifiers that are labeled as "orthodontic" or "orthodontically correct."

Busy hands are happy hands. Dr. Turner recommends taking advantage of your thumb-sucking toddler's natural desire to explore and learn new ways to use her body by introducing activities that keep her hands busy. Crafts like painting or playing with Play-Doh give her alternate ways to keep her hands busy. Games that involve covering the hands, like playing with puppets, wearing gloves for dress-up, or playing pat-a-cake will all give your toddler a chance to make good use of her hands without putting them in her mouth.

Cheer her on. If your toddler does agree or decide to cut back on the time she uses her pacifier or sucks her thumb, praise any progress she makes and try to ignore any slips in her resolve. The fact that she is willing to think about giving up her habit is progress, but actually doing it may take some time.

Chapter 48

WHY DO TODDLERS DRAG AROUND A FAVORITE BLANKET?

We've all heard of liquid courage. It comes in a shot glass, usually—occasionally in a mug or a wineglass. Toddlers have their own, substantially less toxic, version of this longstanding social crutch; they have their "loveys."

A lovey is what child psychologists call an "attachment object"—something that makes your toddler feel less alone when you're not with her. Toddlers create them and give them their significance because they can control them and use them at the whim of their wills, explains Megan McClelland, Ph.D., associate professor of human development and family sciences at Oregon State University. Usually, loveys start as something nice and soft and snuggly that happened to be in your toddler's crib around the time she turned a year old and started gaining a little independence. Blankets are the most popular models, closely followed by stuffed animals. In a pretty impressive stretch of their young imaginations, some toddlers decide to instill these inanimate objects with special, symbolic meaning. They use their loveys just like they'd use a mom or dad nearby, snuggling with them, rubbing themselves against them, falling asleep with them in their hands.

The reason toddlers give all that credence to otherwise average blankets and teddy bears is that they need a little extra courage and comfort to bolster them as they learn to face the world on their own two feet, or alone in the crib, rather than from the security of their parents' arms.

As a whole, our society tends to frown on social crutches, deeming the Linuses of the world as insecure and needy. The fact is, though, that children who create and depend on loveys are quite a self-sufficient group, a fact demonstrated by the research of Richard Passman, Ph.D., a psychology professor at the University of Wisconsin at Milwaukee, over the past thirty years. Dr. Passman and his colleagues have studied toddlers with security objects in all kinds of different circumstances, and they have consistently found that the approximately thirty percent of toddlers who rely on loveys are just as well-adjusted as their peers who do not have them.

What has been most notable in Dr. Passman's research, though, is that when toddlers were tested in stressful situations like classrooms, doctor's offices, and new play areas with their mothers, with their loveys, with neither, and with both, kids who had their loveys along were just as comfortable and confident as those who were with Mom.

The fact that small children can assign so much emotional significance to any one object and then believe in it so completely is one of the wonders of their intellectual and cognitive growth.

💡 NOW THAT YOU KNOW

Little things mean a lot. Even the researchers who know loveys best are still not clear about why some toddlers take on attachment items and others don't seem to need them. There is widespread agreement, though, that loveys serve a critical purpose in some children's early development. Alicia Lieberman, Ph.D., professor of psychology at the University of California at San Francisco and author of *The Emotional Life of the Toddler,* writes: "the most important emotional accomplishment of the toddler years is reconciling the urge to become competent and self-reliant with the longing for parental love and protection." For some kids, there is no more efficient tool for getting from that point A to point B than the use of an attachment object.

All in good time. Children do eventually give up their loveys, but there is no reason to push your toddler to do so anytime soon. In fact, as you read this, you may be thinking of your own long-put-away lovey, sitting on a closet shelf or tucked away in a box in the attic. If your toddler doesn't have to give up her attachment object to conform to the rules of a child care program, there's no need to try to interfere with your child's relationship with it until she's well into her preschool years.

We'll have none of that here. If the daycare provider or mother's day out program you choose absolutely won't allow your toddler to bring her lovey to school, you may want to reconsider sending her there. If you're sure it's the right place, see if your toddler can live with bringing her lovey in the car or stroller and knowing it will be waiting for her when she gets picked up.

Washing: all or nothing. If you see your toddler starting to lean heavily on a particular washable item for comfort, you've got to make a decision: either this is something you wash regularly, or something you don't wash at all. If you start right away, your toddler may go ahead and become attached to a clean-smelling blanket, and as long as you give it a quick wash at regular intervals, the clean smell will be one she can live with. If you do not wash the blanket as your toddler becomes more deeply attached, you may have to live with it dirty. Toddlers are very attuned to the smells of their favorite things, and some become nearly as upset upon discovering that their beloved lovey now smells like laundry detergent as they would if they'd lost it altogether.

No substitutes. One of the surprising facts to be discovered in research about toddlers and their loveys is that many are more upset to be offered a substitute for their beloved cuddle object than they are to have to muddle through without one at all.

Don't have one? Do you need one? Some parents try to help their young toddlers establish a relationship with a lovey because they can help resolve sleep issues. If you're going to deliberately set about giving your child a lovey, buy a duplicate right from the start. Choose an object that has an appealing texture for your toddler and that is not too large or heavy—quilt-sized loveys, for example, can be a physical burden for toddlers who think they need to carry them around. If you rock or nurse your child before bed, bring the lovey along. Put the lovey in her crib for a few nights, then start trying to put it in her hands as you help her fall asleep. Eventually, if the lovey is a part of the bedtime routine, your toddler may learn to more easily fall asleep on her own with the help of her newfound security blanket.

Chapter 49

WHY DO TODDLERS SAY "NO, NO, NO"?

It is the word of the day, the word of the week, the word of the month, and the word of the year. It is notoriously popular among two-year-olds, but beloved by ones and threes, too. It is the word "no," and if you listen closely to the ways your toddler uses it, you'll find that in addition to its traditional meaning, "no" can also mean "never," "not right now," "not while you're watching," "not if you want me to," and sometimes, "yes."

A bad case of no usually starts soon after your toddler starts walking, and gains popularity for many months thereafter. The timing makes perfect sense, explains Alice Sterling Honig, Ph.D., professor emerita of child development at Syracuse University. Toddlers are struggling to gain a sense of autonomy, and their first real physical freedom—being able to walk and climb and move their bodies at will—helps them take great strides toward independence. Once they experience some physical control, though, toddlers move quickly forward to wanting to prove they have psychological and social power, too.

Ready to express themselves, toddlers rifle through the limited arsenal of vocabulary available to them—for some as few as fifty words in their mental dictionaries, for even the most advanced a fraction of what the average adult can use—for a phrase that demonstrates their power and independence. Few words hold the kind of power to gain attention, accomplish self-expression, and establish autonomy like "no." Toddlers almost universally agree on it as the word of choice.

Dr. Honig points out that the use of no gets another boost from even the most well-intentioned parents during this phase. "Since increased physical activity and curiosity is helping your toddler to climb on mama's dresser or on the kitchen counter at this time, most toddlers are hearing a lot of sharp no's from their parents," Dr. Honig explains. "Toddlers are the world's greatest imitators."

When a toddler finds "no," a whole new world opens up for her. Suddenly, she does not, will not, can not—she is the master of her own, albeit very negative, fate. She's an independent woman, so to speak. The power of throwing around those early negatives is borderline addictive.

"Sometimes toddlers are so pleased with themselves for saying no, they'll grin up at the grown-up as if they've just won a great personal victory," says Dr. Honig, even if the toddler actually did want what was offered, or wanted to do what the adult requested. When they answer "No" to "Are you ready for lunch?" or "Would you like to take a walk now?" toddlers lose out on things that hold great appeal for them. Many say it anyway, though, because for this brief time, the thrill of asserting themselves in telling us what they do not want outweighs everything else.

NOW THAT YOU KNOW

Take them at their word. The great thing about toddlers' over-enthusiasm with their use of no, is that sometimes you don't have to do anything but listen for them to learn they'd better use it with care. If your toddler shouts "No" when asked if he'd like a snack, or to play a game, just say, "Okay," and see if they come around. Parents often make the mistake of forcing good things on their little naysayers instead of letting them think for a bit about what they've just said.

Another way to have a say. To help jog your toddler past the no stage, stop asking questions to which the word is a sensible answer. You will get "No" as a reply sometimes anyway—conversations don't always have to make perfect sense as far as your toddler is concerned—but more often than not, if you ask a question that requires a different answer, you'll get one.

The best approaches to toddlers at this age are questions that give them two choices to pick from. It is your acknowledgment that your toddler has a right to his opinion—the lesson he's trying to get across by throwing no around so much anyway—but it lets you have some influence over the outcome. Instead of asking your toddler if he wants toast, ask whether he wants toast or cereal. Instead of, "Put on your white shoes," say "Which would you like to put on, the white shoes or the blue ones?"

Set a good example. When you're trying to help your toddler find other ways to express himself besides "No, no, no," it helps if you use the offending word as little as possible yourself. Find other ways to say what you need to. "When you see your child running, don't say 'Don't run,'" explains Dr. Honig, "say 'Walk slowly, honey!' or 'Walk carefully!' Use as much positive language as you possibly can. Use words like 'gently' and 'carefully' a zillion times a day."

In short, the fewer sharp no's your toddler hears from you, the fewer you're likely to hear back.

Turn the other ear. The less of a rise your toddler gets out of you when she gives you a big, loud "NO," the better. There is no greater reinforcement for a toddler who is trying to prove to herself she has some power in this world to keep saying no than to see she can make her mom's hair stand on end when she does it. When you've been lobbed a gratuitous no, and there's no critical conversation hanging on it, just pretend you didn't hear. Ignoring the no will help cut down on the problem.

Teach yes. It's good that your toddler has discovered the many wonders of using no. But it is also time for her to learn there are other words that show she has a preference, too. Oftentimes, new turns of phrase are most easily learned if you introduce them in play. Sit down with your toddler for a tea party, for example, and invite some of her stuffed animals to join you. As you ask each if it would like tea, use a different voice to give a positive response: "Why, yes, that would be lovely"; "Certainly I would like some tea"; "How sweet of you to ask, darling, I do like tea"; "Sure, your cookies are always delicious." Your toddler will be in giggles about her overly polite guests, but she'll also start thinking about the fact that yes is, in fact, a viable answer.

Chapter 50

WHY DO TODDLERS THINK EVERYTHING IS "MINE, MINE, MINE"?

The problem, in a nutshell, is this: before toddlers turn two, they understand the concept of ownership. You'll know it when they reach this milestone, because you'll be hearing a great deal of their new second-favorite word (after "no"): "mine." The fact that your toddler has reached this developmental mark is a lovely accomplishment. Mother Nature has a quirky sense of humor, though. While your toddler can understand "mine" by age twenty months or soon after, she won't begin to grasp what it means to share for *at least* another year.

For toddlers, that means a year or more of establishing and developing their sense of ownership over every last thing in their lives, pretty much unchecked. For parents, it means the sometimes shocking realization that your child is selfish, greedy, or both. You may be amazed to discover just how all-encompassing some toddlers' scope of "mine" can be. Of course, all his toys are "mine." All his siblings' toys are "mine," too. The food in the fridge, the car in the driveway, the swing at the park, all "mine."

When your toddler informs you that the song you are singing, the jewelry on your fingers, and the family dog belong to him, too, you may begin to wonder just what kind of monster you are raising.

"Even though sometimes it's hard for parents to accept, there is a developmentally appropriate time for children to be selfish, and this is it," explains Tovah Klein, Ph.D., director of the Barnard Center for Toddler Development of Barnard College.

Until your child is at least two-and-a-half, and probably not until after he's three, trying to teach actual sharing is going to be a waste of time. Until then, says Dr. Klein, it's best to respect your toddler's sense of absolute propriety over his own things and not push the issue. Forcing him to share before he can grasp the concept will make him more, not less, possessive.

Instead, try to gradually open your child's eyes to the fact that just like some things belong to him, there are things that belong to other people. This is an especially important lesson if you have other children, because the mine phase is often the one during which strife between older siblings and toddler brothers and sisters can start to get ugly over possessions.

In the beginning, your toddler will not be able to distinguish between what is his and what is not, so don't ever get into a verbal battle over who owns what with your toddler. Just matter-of-factly tell him when he is encroaching on someone else's belongings, and help him move on to something else. If the person who owns the object of your toddler's affection is willing to share, be sure you tell him so and help him return the object. If you have older children who are willing to do this for the toddler in the family, be sure to thank them and affirm their behavior yourself. It's easy for even more mature big kids to fall into thinking the toddler is Mom's or Dad's favorite if they are asked to cave in for him too often.

⏀ NOW THAT YOU KNOW

Give a demonstration. There's nothing you can do to erase the lag between owning and sharing, but you can help prepare your child for future sharing by making a point of doing it for him. Tell him what you are doing—"Would you like to share my cookie with me?" or "We can share this snuggly blanket"—so the word, and the concept, begin to be a part of his vocabulary and experience.

Handle with care. Once toddlers hit the mine stage, they can be very aggressive in asserting their ownership over the things they want. What doesn't seem like a big issue when your toddler does it to you can be huge when it's another toddler who has the thing he's decided is his. Sadly, toddler play dates are not really the coffee-drinking, cookie-eating affairs us moms deserve. They are social situations in which hovering over your toddler (or at least watching *very* closely) is a necessary evil to prevent kicking, hitting, hair-pulling, and the like. Don't be surprised if your toddler is willing to get physical to take what he wants, but don't condone it, either. A firm "No, we don't take things from our friends," and a quick, quiet time-out is usually enough to settle things down. Unfortunately, if your toddler goes back for the same item after being removed from the situation once, it's probably time for the two of you to go home. Don't lose your temper over this kind of incident, because they happen to all of us. Just end the situation for today and hope for better behavior next time.

Keep it if you want to. You may be mortified when your toddler refuses to share even a single toy with a playmate, or to show his new toy to a family friend, but the less attention you pay to the greedy side, the better. If you let them hoard their toys for a while, the sociable side of most toddlers eventually gets the best of them. They will allow—or invite—other people to play with them when they're ready.

A time to give in, even when it's yours, yours, yours. If your toddler is hungry, tired, sick, or otherwise heading toward an emotional train wreck, it's okay to occasionally give in and let him take possession of things that aren't his (provided he's not taking them from another hungry, tired, sick or emotionally wound-up toddler, of course). Sometimes it seems we worry so much about spoiling our children that we unintentionally end up in a battle of wills with them. When your toddler starts staking his claim, but *before* he gets to the point of a major whine or temper tantrum, tell him you're going to lend him the thing he wants if you can. Say, "You know, I think I'll let you borrow that," and do so. I've loaned my children my jewelry, my glasses, and even the keyboard from my computer for short periods of time, and averted major crises when they were overtired or sick. It's part of the maturity of being a parent that sometimes you can decide it's in everyone's best interest to keep the peace by whatever means necessary.

Chapter 51

WHY DO SOME TODDLERS
FEAR EVERYTHING?

Most parents know what it's like when a toddler cowers behind their legs, clinging for dear life. It makes you feel strong, protective, needed, and loved.

But if your toddler hides behind you all the time, if she doesn't seem to be moving past her fears and shyness like her peers, if she can't enjoy visiting new places or seeing new things, then what was flattering can become a source of worry and irritation. How could your child be so insecure? Did you make her that way?

Chances are, if you contributed to the insecurity of a young toddler, it was through your genetic donation, and not in the dynamics of your parenting. Recent research by Harvard University professor Jerome Kagan, Ph.D., strongly suggested that the kind of temperaments we call shy, fearful, or inhibited can be inherited. Shy toddlers have real, measurable differences from their outgoing peers in the way their brains process changes in the environment.

Studies suggest that as many as one in seven children have inherited shyness, so if your toddler is one who is easily intimidated by the world, rest assured she is not alone. Having a toddler who seems to have been born with a high level of anxiety and fearfulness presents unique challenges—among others, trying to find a way to reassure without being overprotective, and acknowledging your child's fears without making them worse. It may be predetermined that on a scale from one to ten, your child will land somewhere between seven and ten in terms of how shy, nervous, and fearful she is in her childhood—perhaps in her entire life, explains Edward Christophersen, Ph.D., clinical psychologist and professor of pediatrics at the University of Missouri at Kansas City School of Medicine and author of *Parenting That Works: Building Skills That Last a Lifetime*. That range, however, is all that is set in stone. "Whether your child ends up at the seven, the ten, or somewhere in between is much more within your control," says Dr. Christophersen.

A research experiment with monkeys who displayed early fearful, shy behavior supports Dr. Christophersen's assertions. Scientists placed fearful infant monkeys with mother monkeys that were known to be experienced, nurturing parents. Over time, not only did the shy young monkeys overcome their fears, but they flourished in social situations.

Dr. Kagan's research at Harvard has followed shy toddlers into adulthood and suggests something similar to the primate study: as adults, men and women who were shy two-year-olds still have the physiological response to new stimulus that they had as children—their brains still react to change in a different way than those of their peers. However, it took a brain scan to show that they still had that "shyness effect." Nothing in the behavior of some of the subjects, now successful, outgoing adults, betrayed their shy past.

NOW THAT YOU KNOW

Save the labels. "One of the beauties of working with very young children is that most of the standard measures don't go down as low as this age—things like the assessments for anxiety and depression are not designed to be used for toddlers," says Dr. Christophersen. It's fine to privately discuss your child's fearful nature with your spouse, your family, or the toddler's teacher or doctor, but telling people your toddler is "a scaredy-cat" or even just saying "she's shy" when she's listening can teach her to view herself that way. Keep your discussions with your child about her fears centered in the moment with statements about how she's feeling right now ("Is that dog scaring you?"), but don't overstate the issue and set her up to be afraid again the next time with more generalized comments ("You're scared of dogs, aren't you?").

They have enough to worry about. In their efforts to calm their children's fears, well-meaning parents sometimes make them worse, says Dr. Christophersen. For example, if your child is going to Grandma's house, you might tell her a day or two before, ask her to help you pack her overnight bag, tell her on the way about a fun activity Grandma has planned, and kiss her goodbye when you arrive. Alternatively, you could start setting her up for the trip two weeks in advance, telling her that she will be staying at Grandma's house *all by herself* for *a whole night*. You could tell her two or three times a day between now and the big day that she will *be very safe and have fun* with Grandma.

Unfortunately, your good intentions may backfire, because your repeated assertions that your child will be just fine get her worrying that she might not be fine at all. Dr. Christophersen likens parents' sometimes overzealous approach to preparing and reassuring their children to a situation between adults: "How would you feel if your spouse left for every business trip by reassuring you, 'You don't have to worry about me, honey; I am not going to be unfaithful on this trip.' All that 'reassurance' might just make you worry."

Small steps to success. The key to helping your toddler overcome many fears is finding every last reserve of patience you've got and letting her adjust at her pace. For toddlers, this often means literally working closer and closer to an object they fear, consistently ending the exposure before the child feels any negative response. In one extreme case, for example, Dr. Christophersen treated a young girl who would throw up on the way to preschool every morning. (Dad thought it was "all in her head" until she christened his Lincoln one morning.) The psychologist had the child's mother drive her to the school's parking lot three times a day for a week, then go home. The next week, mother and daughter got out of the car each time, walked up to the door of the school, touched it, then turned around and went home. "Baby steps" takes on new meaning for parents of fearful children, but if you are able to put in the time and energy to help your child see and feel for herself—instead of being told by you—that her fears can be addressed, both of you will reap the benefits of that effort for a lifetime.

Take me as I am. Providing a sense of security for your fearful child, right from birth, is the first key in helping her develop to her full potential. As tiresome as it may get, letting a shy child hide behind your legs when she needs to is part of what she needs from you. If you can stay calm, loving, cheerful, patient, strong, and reassuring during the toddler years, over the long run, your fearful child will start to find the calm, loving, cheerful, patient, strong person within herself.

Chapter 52

WHY DO SOME TODDLERS FEAR NOTHING AT ALL?

Anthony was a gem of a toddler—eager, amiable, affectionate, resilient, always with a big grin on his face. He was also part madman. In his first four years in this world, he did all the things parents go to bed every night praying their toddlers will not do: he put his finger in the sockets; he dangled perilously off the balcony; he touched the stove; he ran in the street. Everyone in his life was consumed with looking out for this child: his parents, his siblings, the babysitter, even strangers who saw from the gleam in his eye that there was a dangerous moment coming soon. Though he suffered a minor electrical shock, a broken arm, and a near-miss to being hit by a car, Anthony survived and grew up to be an intelligent, sensitive, outgoing young man—and in a fitting end to his childhood, he took up running, racing miles each day to nowhere in particular, finally having found an appropriate way to burn all that energy.

In some ways, fearless toddlers—who are often outgoing, physical, who-needs-twelve-hours-of-sleep toddlers as well—are the biggest challenge to parents. They need you desperately, but they run from moment to moment as if they don't need anyone at all. Their courage fills you with pride, but it'll overwhelm you with exhaustion, too. Their determination to do new things doesn't ever seem to be the least bit inhibited by the fact that they don't know how. All of our children make us hold our breath from time to time, but parents of fearless children have to make a concerted effort to exhale.

According to Alice Sterling Honig, Ph.D., professor emerita of child development at Syracuse University, some toddlers just come by their reckless temperaments naturally. In other cases, they adopt them because they are looking for more attention and attachment with their parents. In either case, the best ways to handle the situation come down to parenting with lots of attention and understanding, and setting limits to help keep your child from hurting himself.

A fearless, reckless toddler needs your help to learn to respect the boundaries of his body. "Stroke your child, cuddle him on your lap every day, kiss him and stroke his hair, to help him become more aware of his body and its limits," says Dr. Honig.

In addition to increasing body awareness in your toddler, work on increasing his ability to get himself out of a jam. "Explain cause and effect to your child," Dr. Honig advises. "For example, tell him, 'If you climb up on that tall ledge and jump off, then your legs could get hurt. Let's try jumping off a low ledge first.' Get on the step with him, and help him practice bending his knees and making small jumps. Teach him a safe way to do the things he is going to do anyway."

The approach seems to be based in an if-you-can't-beat-'em mentality, but it has twofold benefits. First, it shows your toddler that you respect the fact that he is a fast, physical individual. Second, by prepping him in the realities of the situations he gets into, you prepare him to appraise them and safely handle himself.

When it comes time to applaud your toddler's efforts, be sure to save your praise for activities that show he's remembering his limitations. Even if he walks away from a reckless move without a scratch, try to keep your reaction low key. The attention will encourage a repeat performance, and your toddler may not be as lucky the next time.

☀️ NOW THAT YOU KNOW

Rules are rules. For all toddlers, but especially for fearless ones, a few simple, non-negotiable rules to keep them safe are essential. Tell your toddler, right from the beginning, that breaking "safety rules" will not be tolerated, and follow through immediately if they are broken with a firm reminder and a short time-out. Be sure your safety rules include a ban on rough play with other toddlers and unsafe climbing.

Just as important as safety rules are opportunities for your wild child to put his abundance of energy to good use. Kids with fearless personalities need lots of time for physical play, outdoor play, and for exploring new things. Having those outlets at regular intervals can make the difference between raising an active, busy toddler and raising one who seems uncontrollable.

Play along. You'll quickly find that the best way to connect with your fearless toddler is to throw yourself into physical play with him. Being a playmate for a one-, two-, or three-year-old can be exhausting, but it'll raise your profile in your toddler's eyes. When he sees that he can sometimes follow your lead in the activities he enjoys most, it can make it easier for him to cooperate and trust you in other, less playful, situations.

Brag not. Raising a fearless toddler is bound to arm you with a string of exciting events that need to be reported to family and friends. Unless you want to encourage your toddler's reckless behavior, though, don't discuss it with other people in front of him. Hearing about his own dramatic exploits after the fact will make him even more daring the next time around.

Draw your discipline line. In raising a fearless child, many parents resort to dramatic discipline—including shouting and spanking. It's an easy trap to fall into, especially when you're afraid for your child's safety.

The danger in either is that you risk losing your own temper, and that you teach your already excitable child to react that way, too. "I just got my pilot's license, and in the process of learning, I made a lot of mistakes," says Edward Christophersen, Ph.D., clinical psychologist and professor of pediatrics at the University of Missouri at Kansas City School of Medicine and author of *Parenting That Works: Building Skills That Last a Lifetime*, "but my instructor never once yelled at me or slapped me. We can work miracles with our children without hurting them, too."

In place of physical discipline, Dr. Christophersen recommends two alternate courses of action. First, use time-outs consistently. Time-out should involve as little conversation as possible, he explains. Tell your toddler what he is doing that has to stop—"we do not climb on the counter"—and remove him from all activity for a few minutes (five or less). Second, teach your child alternate ways to get your attention, to amuse himself, and to expend his energy.

Find a good mom. When the parenting road gets rough, one of the best things you can do for yourself is to find other parents who are doing a great job, and take a hard look at what works for them. As Dr. Christophersen explains, "You can learn more in a single afternoon with an experienced, composed, loving mom who relates well to her children than I can tell you in a lifetime."

Conclusion

THE BEST ADVICE

New moms are inundated with advice on everything from the best place to shop for baby clothes to the best method for getting a burp out of an unwilling infant. As our children hit their toddler years, the advice keeps coming, and sometimes it seems to take on a more critical edge. (Do we really need anyone to tell us we'd better get our child's biting habit under control? Do we not feel the pressure to accomplish toilet training enough without having to endure the "how to" advice of every parent whose child beat ours to it?)

As a mom and journalist who has interviewed dozens of early childhood specialists, I've been on the receiving end of more than my share of parenting advice. The following ten suggestions are the best of the bunch. They have helped me not just manage, but truly enjoy, my children's toddler years. I hope they do the same for you.

1. If you say you're going to do something, you have to do it. Teaching your toddler to take you at your word may be the most important step in paving a smooth path through early childhood. With this in mind, choose your threats carefully when you're considering punishments, and make your promises sin-

cerely when you say you're going to read a book or take time to play with your toddler. If you do both, your child will learn that you can be trusted and counted on, and that security—both in discipline and in everything else—will be a cornerstone of a stable parent/child relationship for years to come.

2. If you want your children to treat other people with respect and consideration, model that behavior at home. Good manners and courtesy come easily to toddlers who see and hear them every day.

3. Losing your temper with a toddler teaches that toddler how to lose his temper, too. Everyone gets angry, but it's your responsibility to show your toddler that there are other ways to deal with that emotion than the ones—like kicking, screaming, and stomping his feet—that he's inevitably going to try out on his own. When you get mad, tell your toddler you're angry, tell him why, and tell him what you're going to do to make yourself feel better. You don't have to sugarcoat it, but you can explain to your toddler that something like going for a walk or spending a few minutes alone in your room helps make you feel better.

4. If your child is doing something you don't like, don't laugh, don't cry, and don't talk about it in front of him. Toddlers are preprogrammed to seek attention. If yours is getting it—even in the form of hearing you talk about his bad behavior with friends and family—the behavior in question is going to crop up again.

5. Contrary to what we all learned in college, children are not blank slates. They come into this world with personalities very much their own. If you respect the fact that part of your toddler's character is wired in and work with, not against, those early indications of her personality, things will go easier for everyone involved.

6. Let your toddler try. There's a fine line between shielding your toddler from danger and frustration and smothering him. Unless there's an immediate danger, let your child climb the stairs, pick up the big rock, step in the puddle, and try a little longer to put together the puzzle himself. He needs a chance to discover his limitations, his strengths, and his ability to make things happen on his own.

7. No parent is perfect. When you make a mistake with your toddler, own up to it and apologize. Almost every toddler is willing to forgive.

8. You get two big windows of opportunity in your life to do stuff like build castles, step in puddles, watch *Sesame Street* and just plain play: the first when you *are* a child, the second when you *have* one. Don't get too busy or wrapped up in the grown-up stuff to miss it.

9. Take a time-out. Small children may hear the words "time out" with dread, but adults know this is not a bad thing. Setting aside time for yourself—for a walk, a bath, or even just a haircut—is just as important as making time for those things for your child.

10. Watch them while they're sleeping. A day with a toddler who's acting like a tyrant is enough to wear on the nerves of a saint. When you hit a rough patch with your child, try tiptoeing in to watch her sleep for a few minutes before you go off to bed. When they're screaming or throwing the dishes from the toy tea set, toddlers may seem powerful and miserable beyond their years; but when they're sleeping, you can't help but be reminded of how vulnerable, small, utterly beautiful, and needy they are.

Appendix A

TIME-OUTS FOR TODDLERS

Some of the behaviors in this book call for using that loosely-defined parental strategy known as a "time-out." There are so many variations on this theme, it can be hard to figure out what, exactly, you're supposed to do with your toddler during a time-out, and when, exactly, you ought to use one.

In truth, in the years since it was first conceived as a means of behavior modification by legendary psychologist B. F. Skinner in the 1960s, the concept of time has become barely recognizable from where it began. Back then, it was called "time out from positive reinforcement"—and it was something Dr. Skinner was trying out not on children, but on pigeons. Basically, it involved turning off the lights in the "Skinner boxes" in which the pigeons were kept to stop them from continuing a particular behavior.

Today, time-out is a disciplinary hot-button for parents and parenting experts, with some swearing by the effectiveness of one of its many forms, and others writing it off as cruel, unreasonable, or just too complicated for toddlers to understand.

According to Edward Christophersen, Ph.D., clinical psychologist and professor of pediatrics at the University of Missouri at Kansas City School of Medicine, time-out can be an effective tool for parents of kids at any age—as long as we keep in mind that its function is not to punish a behavior, but to take away the positive reinforcement that goes along with it.

For toddlers, time-out should boil down to removing your child from the scene of a behavior problem and withdrawing your attention. For most toddlers, this is done best *without* the use of a time-out chair. The problem with time-out chairs for kids this age is that toddlers are notoriously bad at sitting in chairs at any time. When they're angry and in trouble with Mom or Dad, things get worse. If you insist that your toddler stay still, bottom in chair, for any length of time, you're setting yourself up for a disciplinary incident that becomes all about your child's physical position relative to the chair, and is deeply frustrating for both of you. In a flurry of "You will sit in this chair. Stay in that chair. I told you to stay in your chair for two minutes," and so on, it may soon become unclear if it's you or your little one who's being punished.

Instead of associating time-out with a prescribed number of minutes in a specific spot, use the concept as it fits your toddler's situation. Follow these guidelines to make the concept work for your family.

- *Interrupt.* Time-out should only be used as a response to undesirable behavior, so the first step in any time-out is bringing that behavior to a halt.

- *Talk is cheap.* When you interrupt your toddler's bad behavior, do so using the simplest, clearest terms possible. Remember, you're reasoning with an unsophisticated, and most likely overstimulated, mind. Tell your toddler, in a firm, low, clear tone of voice, for example, "No. We do not hit. Time-out," and leave it at that.

- *Change the scene.* Your toddler needs to get away from the environment that fostered the bad behavior in the first place. Whether you take your toddler to the corner, to another room, or to a place outside doesn't matter much. What is important is that he has a sense of being removed from the scene of the problem. If you have carried him to the new spot, put your toddler down and calmly repeat, "You need a time-out." Then avert your eyes, step away, and don't speak to him. Your attention is the biggest thing you have to take away.

- *Keep your cool.* When you get to your time-out spot, don't blow up at your toddler, don't try to hold him in one place, and don't give a lecture about this being a punishment. Simply wait quietly.

- *How long does it take?* Time-out only takes as long as it takes for your child to settle down and cease to be agitated. It may be less than a minute; it may be two minutes or four. As soon as you see your toddler begin to relax, it should be over. Remind him once more of the transgression that started the whole thing, tell him you're sure he won't do it again, and then either move on to the next activity or go back to the previous one.

- *Use sparingly.* Save time-outs for when you really need them—for when it's too late to redirect your toddler to another activity, or when things have gone so far that your toddler needs to know he's done something wrong. Time-out is not an all-purpose method for dealing with behavior issues, but when used properly, it can certainly help.

Appendix B

RESOURCES

RECOMMENDED CHILD DEVELOPMENT AND BEHAVIOR BOOKS FOR PARENTS

Einstein Never Used Flashcards: How Our Children Really Learn, and Why They Need to Play More and Memorize Less
By Kathy Hirsh-Pasek, Ph.D., and Roberta Michnick Golinkoff, Ph.D., with Diane Eyer, Ph.D.
(Rodale Press, 2003)

Magic Trees of the Mind: How to Nurture Your Child's Intelligence, Creativity, and Healthy Emotions from Birth through Adolescence
By Marian Diamond, Ph.D., and Janet Hopson
(Penguin Group (USA), 1999)

Parenting That Works: Building Skills That Last a Lifetime
By Edward Christophersen, Ph.D., and Susan Mortweet, Ph.D.
(American Psychological Association, 2002)

The Scientist in the Crib: What Early Learning Tells Us About the Mind
By Alison Gopnik, Ph.D., Andrew N. Meltzoff, Ph.D., and Patricia Kuhl, Ph.D.
(William Morrow and Company, Inc., 1999)

Sleeping Through the Night: How Infants, Toddlers and Their Parents Can Get a Good Night's Sleep
By Jodi Mindell, Ph.D.
(HarperResource, 1997)

What's Going On in There? How the Brain and Mind Develop in the First Five Years of Life
By Lise Elliot, Ph.D.
(Bantam, 1999)

RECOMMENDED BOOKS ABOUT LIFE WITH TODDLERS FOR PARENTS

The Girlfriends' Guide to Toddlers
By Vicki Iovine
(Perigee, 1999)

Preschool Confidential
By Sandi Kahn Shelton
(St. Martin's Press, 2001)

RECOMMENDED POTTY TRAINING RESOURCES FOR TODDLERS

My Big Boy Potty/My Big Girl Potty
By Joanna Cole and Maxie Chambliss
(HarperCollins, 2000)

The New Potty
By Gina Mayer
(Golden Books, 2003)

Potty Time
By Bettina Paterson
(Grosset & Dunlap, 1993)

The Princess and the Potty
By Wendy Lewison and Rick Brown
(Aladdin Library, 1998)

Bear in the Big Blue House: Potty Time with Bear (VHS or DVD)
(Columbia/Tristar Studios, 2002)

RECOMMENDED WEB SITES FOR PARENTS

www.babycenter.com
Babycenter features hundreds of well-written, well-researched articles for parents. Despite the "baby" name, a large portion of these articles pertain specifically to toddlers.

www.child.com
The *Child* magazine Web site features sophisticated, thoughtful parenting articles about children of all ages.

www.drgreene.com
There are hundreds and hundreds of articles, photos, and FAQs with accessible, straight-talking information and advice from this internationally respected pediatrician on his site. Dr. Greene and associates tackle everything from allergies and asthma to potty training and sleep issues. The site covers infancy through adolescence, and is worth a bookmark on every parent's computer.

www.earlychildhood.com
This early childhood site is not as comprehensive as some of the others listed here, but it contains an excellent Ask the Expert section that intelligently and compassionately addresses many of the issues parents of toddlers deal with.

www.eric.ed.gov
The Educational Resources Information Center is primarily designed for educators, but it is a wealth of information about education-related topics for parents of children of all ages. The site is especially helpful for parents of children with disabilities, as it contains many reports written specifically about those children's needs.

www.naturalchild.com

The Natural Child Project site is not for everyone as it has a distinct political bent, but it has a strong selection of articles on attachment parenting, cosleeping, home education, and the multifaceted nature of intelligence.

www.parents.com

If you're a fan of *Parents* magazine, you'll be happy to find a substantial online collection of As We Grow columns on their Web site. There are tons of well-written articles on this site from top experts in all aspects of parenting.

www.zerotothree.org

Zero to Three is a government-sponsored site with separate sections for parents and for professionals who work with young children. The board which consults for and oversees the content of this site includes many of the most respected early childhood experts in the nation. The resulting site is a collection of informative, interesting, and often definitive articles about raising young children.

Index

About the Author

Jana Murphy is a journalist whose trademarks are in-depth research and an engaging, straightforward tone. Whether she's writing about hot chocolate or hotly disputed trends in child rearing, she goes to the top experts in each field to uncover the facts and presents each topic with honesty, warmth, and detail. Jana writes both books and magazine articles about parenting, pets, cooking, and travel.

Jana has written for *Parents* and *BottomLine Health* and was a contributing author to the books *The Immune Advantage* and *Dr. Mom*. She was the editor of *PetLife Magazine* for three years and is a contributing editor to *Chile Pepper* magazine. Jana is also the author of *The Secret Lives of Dogs* and coauthor of *The Lost Pet Chronicles*.

A mother of three and aunt to twenty-four and counting, Jana lives with her husband and children in Bethlehem, Pennsylvania.